From Ulster to Carolina

This Irish woman, photographed on her farm in Bally Castle, County Antrim, about 1903, is sweeping her yard. Photograph from Library of Congress (LC–USZ62-67983).

From Ulster to Carolina

The Migration of the Scotch-Irish
to Southwestern North Carolina

REVISED EDITION

H. Tyler Blethen and Curtis W. Wood Jr.

Raleigh
North Carolina Department of Cultural Resources
Office of Archives and History

Printed by Edwards Brothers Inc.

Contents

Maps and Illustrations

Foreword

One cannot study the early settlement of North Carolina without exploring the migration of the Scotch-Irish into the colony and state. Known in Ireland as the Ulster Scots, these migrants from the Old World to the New left the indelible stamp of their culture upon North Carolina.

In *From Ulster to Carolina: The Migration of the Scotch-Irish to Southwestern North Carolina*, H. Tyler Blethen and Curtis W. Wood Jr. recount the long trek of the Scotch-Irish from their adoptive Irish homeland to the mountains of southwestern North Carolina. The authors graphically describe the religion, occupations, living conditions, social life, and customs of the Protestant Scots who chose to make new lives in America.

Drs. Blethen and Wood are professors of history at Western Carolina University (WCU) at Cullowhee. They received their doctoral degrees from the University of North Carolina at Chapel Hill and have collaborated on a number of publications, most recently as coeditors of the book *Ulster and North America: Transatlantic Perspectives on the Scotch-Irish* (Tuscaloosa: University of Alabama Press, 1997). Dr. Blethen is also director of the Mountain Heritage Center at WCU, and Dr. Wood is former senior research associate at the center and professor emeritus in the Department of History at the university. They were assisted in the production of this volume by Robert M. Topkins, former head of the General Publications Branch of the Historical Publications Section, who edited the book and saw it through press. Staff editor Lisa D. Bailey proofread the publication. Kenny N. Simpson prepared the index.

From Ulster to Carolina originally appeared in an earlier edition published by Western Carolina University, and the Historical Publications Section gratefully acknowledges that institution's assistance in producing this version of the work.

Donna E. Kelly, *Administrator*
Historical Publications Section

Acknowledgments

This small book was originally written to accompany a major exhibition titled *The Migration of the Scotch-Irish to Southwestern North Carolina*, prepared by the Mountain Heritage Center at Western Carolina University (WCU). We take this opportunity to thank the many people whose generosity and knowledge have made both book and exhibition possible. As we began this project in 1979, it was our good fortune to meet the following scholars in Northern Ireland whose enthusiastic support has been indispensable: Brian Trainor, director of the Public Record Office of Northern Ireland, and his staff; Eric Montgomery, director of the Ulster-American Folk Park, and his staff, especially Dennis MacNeice; George Thompson, director of the Ulster Folk and Transport Museum, and museum staff members William Crawford, Philip Robinson, and Alan Gailey; W. T. Ewing, registrar of the New University of Ulster; Frank Lelievre, formerly of Magee University College; David Hammond of the British Broadcasting Corporation, Belfast; and the director and staff of the Ulster Museum in Belfast.

On this side of the Atlantic we also owe many debts of gratitude: to Henry Glassie of the University of Pennsylvania and Robert Mitchell of the University of Maryland for advice in the early stages of the project; to Cratis Williams and Carrie Lindsay of Appalachian State University; to the staff of the Rockingham County Historical Society of Harrisonburg, Virginia; to the Greensboro Historical Museum, Greensboro; to Old Salem, Inc., Winston-Salem; and to the staff of the Mountain Heritage Center.

We are indebted to the many families with ties to southwestern North Carolina who have shared with us their personal histories. These families are too numerous to list, but we are especially grateful to Col. Walter Cathey, to Dr. James Stewart, to Paul McElroy, and to the Patton family of Macon and Clay counties.

Finally, a special word of thanks goes to our colleagues and students who have contributed to the research and preparation of both book and exhibition, especially Lee Budahl of the WCU art department; Clifford Lovin, former director of the Moutain Heritage Center; Joe Ginn, David Smith, and Keith Patton, who helped keep the WCU history department functioning; and Scott Philyaw, who went to Belfast for us.

H. Tyler Blethen
Curtis W. Wood Jr.

Introduction

From the earliest recorded history, humans have moved across the face of the earth. Migration—the movement of individuals, families, communities, and entire peoples—has been one of the most important human experiences shaping history. It involves leave-taking from one home and one environment in search of another, the crossing of frontiers, rivers, mountains, oceans. The emigrant always takes something of his or her ethnic legacy, something of the old culture and life as a gift to the new land. Equally important, migration also brings fundamental change. A new physical environment—new soil, new climate, new resources—inexorably reshapes the life of the transplanted people. The cultural practices of new people whom emigrants encounter influence their own practices and result in some degree of adaptation. When people move, they take with them what they can, cultural as well as material baggage, but they cannot take everything. The new situation forces them to create new tools and new institutions, built upon what they brought from home but modified to meet the challenges of the new environment. To migrate invariably means to gamble, to risk one's welfare as well as one's cherished customs and beliefs. It requires that community be rebuilt by a transplanted fragment in a new setting.

Some migrants are pushed into their venture with regret, driven by famine, economic hardship, or persecution. Others, more happily, are drawn by hope of a better life. Many are propelled into motion by both forces. With the exception of the vast African migration, which was entirely forced, the diverse peoples who settled colonial America were both pushed and pulled.

The study of migration is particularly significant for Americans, for whether in an ancient past (for Native Americans) or in more recent centuries, all Americans are immigrants. Alexis de Tocqueville observed of early American society that the American "grows accustomed to change." To an amazing degree, we have remained a migratory people, profoundly mobile, moving from city to city and state to state. Once having moved, it was easier to move again and again.

This small book is concerned with a people who in many ways were the epitome of mobility and change. Their very name is itself witness to the fact that they had known more than one home. In Britain and Ireland they were called Ulster Scots, while in America they received a new name, the Scotch-Irish. In the eighteenth century as they joined other new settlers in America, they were exceptional for their restlessness and eagerness to look beyond wherever they might be for something new and better. They were a people remarkable for their openness to change and their willingness to abandon their ethnic heritage. Our intention is not to claim extravagant credit for the Scotch-Irish in the creation of the new American nation, as some authors have done. They were but one new people among many. Nor do we intend to recount the vast saga of the Scotch-Irish migration across America. Rather, we offer an account of their movement from their homeland surrounding the Irish Sea to the southern Appalachian Mountains and, more specifically, to the westernmost counties of North Carolina, including the present-day counties of Buncombe, Cherokee, Clay, Graham, Haywood, Henderson, Jackson, Macon, Madison, Mitchell, Swain, Transylvania, and Yancey. This region, about two-thirds the size of the nine counties that made up the historic province of Ulster in Ireland, is but one of many locales in which the Scotch-Irish pioneered.

Migrants frequently leave only a sketchy historical record. While the great sweep of events might be clear, the details are often lost in the confusion of movement. Many family histories remain incomplete, and often even the names of those who came first are lost. Understanding and evaluating the experience of the Scotch-Irish is made more difficult by the eagerness with which they threw over the culture of the Old World, which might have identified them as a group in America. Nevertheless, their presence still surrounds us in the southern Appalachians in the evidence of family names, in the stamp the Scotch-Irish placed upon the customs of the region, and in lingering family memories. A distinctive feature of the southern Appalachian region is that its relative isolation in the late nineteenth and early twentieth centuries preserved a strong sense of its Scotch-Irish past. We hope that this book will bring a better understanding of that memory and tradition and will illuminate the shared histories of Scotland, Ulster, and southern Appalachia.

1

The First Frontier:
The Scots of Ulster in the
Seventeenth and Eighteenth
Centuries

Ulster and the Borders

Since time immemorial, history and geography have pushed the people of Ulster and the Borders region of lowland Scotland and northern England together. As part of a fringe of Celtic peoples living on the "Atlantic edge" of Europe, the people of Ulster and the Borders spoke related Gaelic languages and practiced a mixed agriculture that strongly emphasized the raising of sheep and cattle, combined with a simple, subsistence tillage of the land. The land itself imposed similar demands upon these upland pastoral people. Frequently rocky and invariably wet, the land provided them the stone, thatch, turf, wool, and fields with which they housed, clothed, warmed, and fed themselves and their families. The hearth was the place where those elements came visibly together and were translated into stories, music, aspirations, and dreams.

From the earliest times, these people had moved back and forth with relative ease across the North Channel of the Irish Sea. The earliest settlers of Scotland were an Irish people known as the Scoti. During the Middle Ages, Scottish kings and noblemen often led their soldiers across this narrow channel in vain attempts to conquer Ireland. Irish chiefs in turn hired Scottish mercenaries ("galloglasses" and "redshanks") to fight in their wars. For a time the greatest of these Scottish warriors, the MacDonnells of Antrim and the Isles, created a kingdom that spanned the North Channel, bringing Ulster and western Scotland under one rule. Before 1600 the entire region had little experience of stable and orderly government and was regarded by its English neighbor as primitive and chaotic.

Map of the British Isles, indicating the area of plantation and the primary routes of migration into Ulster. Map by Jan Davidson.

In the sixteenth century, however, political and religious forces changed the culture of the people of Ulster and the Borders. As English influence expanded northward, people in the Lowlands of western Scotland increasingly spoke English. Secondly, the radical religious teachings of the Protestant reformer John Calvin were introduced into Scotland and quickly brought about fundamental changes in the lives of Lowland Scots. A corrupt and unpopular Catholic Church was swept away by a powerful Presbyterian movement, and with the new church came new attitudes—an emphasis upon the individual conscience, a belief in equality in the eyes of God, a suspicion of authority in religious matters, an insistence upon education, an austere morality, and a burning hatred of the old religion. These changes not only marked a turning point in Scottish history but also profoundly altered the attitudes of Lowlanders toward their Ulster neighbors, who remained Catholic in religion and Gaelic in language. It was in those important respects that a different kind of Scot emerged and made his presence felt in Ireland once again in the early seventeenth century.

Background to Plantation

In 1603 relations among England, Scotland, and Ireland were fundamentally altered when James VI, king of Scotland, inherited the thrones of England and Ireland from Elizabeth I. One ruler now governed all the territory of the British Isles and Ireland. But it was an incomplete government, for James's new Irish subjects remained unruly and defiant despite their defeat at the hands of the English army. James's determination to pacify his new kingdom of Ireland led to his plan for the Plantation of Ulster by Scots and English settlers. James believed that the unruly, "savage," Gaelic-speaking Irish could be brought under control and civilized if a Protestant, English-speaking, and politically loyal population was "planted" in their midst.

This scheme was not a new one. Queens Mary and Elizabeth had sponsored similar efforts in central and southern Ireland but achieved only limited results. Private colonization efforts had also preceded James's Plantation of 1610. In 1605 Hugh Montgomery and James Hamilton, prominent Scots who enjoyed the favor of the new king, were granted lands in County Down to which they brought Scottish settlers, and the McDonalds sponsored Scottish settlement in the glens of Antrim. By 1610 those private plantations

James Stuart, king of Scotland from early childhood and ruler of England, 1603–1625. Under his direction the Plantation of Ulster was begun in 1610. Photograph of James Stuart from Wikimedia Commons.

were well under way and had created a strong Scottish presence along the coastal counties.

In 1607 the two great Ulster chieftains—the earls of Tyrone and Tyrconnell—fled to France rather than live under the peace that had been imposed on them by the English army in 1603. James responded by confiscating their lands, about 3.8 million acres, comprising most of the counties of Armagh, Cavan, Coleraine (later renamed Londonderry), Donegal, Fermanagh, and Tyrone, which he made available for resettlement by Protestant Scots and English. Monaghan was not included in the scheme of Plantation but would in time be settled also. King James developed his idea for plantation with more care and planning than any of his predecessors. But the key to the success of the new plantation lay in the combination of the collapse of Ulster's Gaelic leadership and Scots familiarity with northern Ireland and their willingness to make the short move from their overpopulated homeland.

In a letter to his lord deputy in Ireland, Sir Arthur Chichester, James I explained his intentions in Ulster as "the settling of religion, the introducing [of] civility, order, and government amongst a barbarous and unsubdued people, . . . acts of piety and glory, and worthy always of a Christian prince to endeavor." The king preferred Scots to settle the province because they were "of a middle temper between the English tender and the Irish rude breeding, and a great deal more like to adventure to plant Ulster than the English, it [Ulster] lying far both from the English native land, and more from their humour, while it [Ulster] lies nigh to Scotland, and the inhabitants not so far from ancient Scots manner."—Public Record Office, Northern Ireland

---

The Plantation Era

The lands confiscated from the two Irish earls and turned into the Plantation of Ulster were granted to new owners in three categories, creating a new landholding elite. Scottish and English men of high rank, known as undertakers, received land in amounts of 1,000, 1,500, or 2,000 acres, which they were to rent to English or Scottish tenants. "Servitors," primarily military men or government administrators, were granted estates of similar size and given permission to rent them to the native Irish as well as to Scots and English tenants. And some native Irish were granted estates of between 100 and 200 acres that they could rent to Irish tenants. In addition, the City of London was granted lands to settle in County Coleraine, which the City promptly renamed County Londonderry.

The plantation brought large numbers of Scots and smaller numbers of English settlers to Ulster. By 1619 it is estimated that some 8,000 of these new families had settled in the six plantation counties, and by 1715 perhaps one-third of Ulster's population of 600,000 consisted of Scots. But the native Irish remained in the province because, despite the wishes of the English government, the new settlers found that they often had to rely on the Irish as tenants as well as laborers. Consequently the settlers found themselves living in a hostile environment, and an extraordinarily complex society drawing upon three conflicting yet intermingling traditions—Irish, Scottish, and English—evolved.

An English government report of 1628 explained the early conflict between Irish natives and the new settlers of Ulster: "The Irish, of whom many townships might be formed, do not dwell together in any ordered form, but wander with their cattle all the summer in the mountains, and all the winter in the woods. And until the Irish are settled . . . there is no safety either for their [the settlers'] goods or lives."

In many ways the new settlers were pioneers on a hostile frontier in the seventeenth and early eighteenth centuries. Large areas of Ulster were still heavily forested and required clearing, particularly in eastern Down, the glens of Antrim, the Erne Basin, and northwest of Lough Neagh. Until about 1750 there remained much unsettled land that invited migration and settlement. Above all, the circumstances of the land seizure ensured that the majority of the Ulster population remained hostile to the newcomers. To protect against that hostility, the new plantation towns of Ulster were walled and fortified. Each undertaker was expected to build within three years a fortified estate house and bawn (fortified courtyard). The Ulster Scots' sense of being a minority surrounded by hostile natives was very strong. It discouraged them from assimilating with the Gaelic Irish and created a defensive frame of mind that outsiders have often remarked upon throughout their subsequent history.

The People and the Land

Most of the settlers from Scotland and England came either as tenants who rented their lands from undertakers, servitors, or the City of London grantees or as landless agricultural laborers who worked for the tenants. Land was rented for a term of twenty-one or thirty-one years or for "three lives" (the lives of three specified people, typically the tenant, his son, and his son's heir). The settlers' major concern was to improve their economic standing, and so they sought the best land available at the lowest rents. Throughout the seventeenth century land was plentiful, and rents were low. Consequently there was continuous migration into Ulster, primarily from Scotland, as well as a great deal of movement by settlers within the province as they sought to improve their holdings. Tenants would often let their leases expire, and in some cases even abandon them, in their search for land of better quality.

"The parts of Scotland nearest to Ireland sent over abundance of people and cattle that filled the counties of Ulster that lay next to the sea; and albeit amongst these, Divine Providence sent over some worthy persons for birth, education and parts, yet the most part were such as either poverty, scandalous lives, or at the best, adventurous seeking of better accommodation, set forward that way. . . . Little care had by any to plant religion."—Life of Mr. Robert Blair *(a minister who was appointed to the Ulster parish of Bangor in 1623)*, Public Record Office, Northern Ireland

---

Lowland areas, and lands only lightly forested, were the most desirable. Where settlers found forests, they cut them down, selling the wood for fuel or lumber and cultivating the land for crops. The hardy Scots, accustomed to poverty, hard labor, and land of the sort they found in Ulster, were well suited to the work at hand and proved more likely than their English neighbors to move about within Ulster in search of better lands.

Ulster Agriculture

Traditional practices of upland pastoral agriculture were common to Scotland and Ulster. The two regions shared similar agricultural resources: simple tools (essentially the spade and an inefficient plow) and an abundance of land best suited to pasture. In Scotland, animals, especially cattle and sheep, were grazed on most of the land. In summer they were herded to pastures on the hills, and large numbers were slaughtered in the fall because there was not enough feed to keep them alive through the winter. Cultivatable land was divided into two parts—the infield and the outfield. Crops, primarily oats, barley, and some wheat, were grown continuously on the infield, nearest the farmhouses and villages. The outfield, farther out, was planted until the soil's fertility decreased, and then it was left fallow for several years to recover.

The "farmtoun" was a distinctive feature of Scottish farming. It consisted of a few families, often related, who rented land from the laird (landlord) in a form of joint tenancy. To ensure equal access to different-quality soils, these families periodically redistributed among themselves the rigs, or raised beds, in

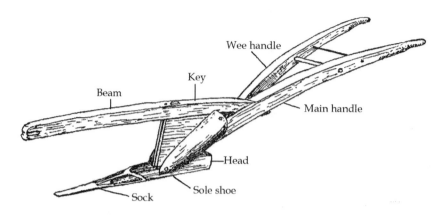

The common wooden plow in eighteenth-century Ulster was very difficult to use and routinely produced furrows that were rarely straight, cleanly dug, or of equal depth. The device was often described as the "old clumsy Irish plough." It "consists of a short head fitted with an iron sock . . . and also shoe with an iron sole-shoe. Into the head is morticed the main handle, in such a way that its left side forms a straight line with the head and with the straight side of the sock. To the main handle are fastened both the wee handle and the long beam which in turn is keyed to the head. . . . Finally a block of wood known as the rest is secured to the right side of the head and has above it a nine-inch mould board. The plough horses had no bits or reins, and the outfit needed two men, one to hold and one to drive. It was often necessary for a third hand to walk alongside the plough, pressing down on the beam with a stout stick." Information from *Irish Heritage: The Landscape, the People and Their Work* (Dundalk: Dundulgan Press, 1958), 89. Drawing from E. E. Evans, *Irish Folkways* (New York: Devin-Adair Company, 1957), 130.

which they planted their crops. This "runrig" or "rundale" pattern of farming encouraged a strong sense of community.

Scotland enjoyed a more productive and settled agriculture than did Ulster before the Plantation. Its economy was more oriented to commercial markets and was managed by powerful lairds. By the seventeenth century, however, access to land in Scotland was increasingly restricted because of a growing population, and Ulster appeared to many land-hungry Scots as an attractive new home in which to practice their traditional agriculture.

The influx of Scots brought by the Plantation did not substantially alter Ulster's patterns of land use because it coexisted comfortably with the Scottish infield-outfield system. A few of the best acres of the farm, often the land that attracted settlement in the first place, and usually near the farm dwellings, became the infield. Crops were grown intensively on it. It received all the farm manure and was never placed in fallow. Infield crops were supplemented by the use of the outfield. The outfield, seldom or never fertilized, was tilled for two or three years in succession and then allowed to lie fallow, often returning to grass or bush and used for pasture. When its soil recovered, it was plowed for crops, and the cycle began again.

The diet of Ulster families was typically supplemented with milk and butter from the livestock grazed on the outfield and on summer upland pastures. From earliest times the poor quality soils of Scotland and Ireland had made raising sheep and cattle a fundamental way of life. Farming still revolved around it in this period. After crops were planted in the spring, the stock either had to be tethered or, more commonly, were driven to graze in rough hill pastures. Often the animals would command more of the time and attention of the farm family or community than did the crops. In late October, after the grain crops were harvested, the livestock were brought back to graze on the stubble left in the infields and outfields. Ulster farming placed emphasis less upon efficiency and high yields and more upon a marginal but sustainable agriculture suited to the conditions of land, tools, and society. The agriculture of Scotland and Ireland contrasted sharply with the intensive cultivation practiced in the prosperous farm villages of southeastern England, and English observers invariably condemned it as primitive and inefficient. In fact, it suited the quality of lands and the demands of markets in the north of Ireland.

Ulster Settlements

Throughout the seventeenth and eighteenth centuries Ulster remained overwhelmingly rural, with little town life. In part that condition resulted from preferences brought by Scottish settlers from the southwestern Lowlands of Scotland who had often lived on scattered farms in farmtouns. Few farmers in Scotland owned land, and tenants often moved in search of more favorable tenancies or were evicted by landlords. It was rare for a family to rent the same farm for more than a single generation.

In Ulster the most common type of settlement was probably the "clachan," or community of joint tenants, who lived in a cluster of dwellings, shared the surrounding land, and worked it together. The clachan was distinctly different from the well-organized agricultural villages found in southeastern England and throughout much of Europe. The former was smaller, typically a community of related families, less regulated by law and custom, more self-sufficient, and less permanent. At least until the middle of the eighteenth century, Ulster still had large areas of unsettled land, and farmers moved frequently.

This clachan, a small, largely self-sufficient community of related families, was a typical form of settlement in seventeenth- and eighteenth-century Ulster. The surrounding land was worked in common. Illustration by Lee Budahl.

Scattered single-family farms also were an important part of Ulster society. Often a family would leave an oversettled clachan, or a clachan would emerge as a family grew and a new community took shape. In the case of both clachan and single-family farm, rural life was more dispersed and individualistic than in most of Europe, but a sense of neighborhood was maintained through kinship ties, church gatherings, and fairs and markets. The picture that emerges from Ulster's past is that of a backward, mixed agriculture practiced by highly mobile and independent farmers. That society provided many of the elements for the life the Ulster Scots developed in their new American home.

Ulster Presbyterianism

Life in the new Ulster society of the seventeenth and eighteenth centuries was profoundly influenced by religion. As there were three ethnic groups (English, Scots, and Irish), so too there were three religious communities (Anglican, Presbyterian, and Catholic). The native Irish people, scattered about the province, limited to inferior lands, and drawn upon for cheap labor, remained

Catholic. Their resentment breathed new life into their religious identity as Catholicism became a symbol of their separate and inferior status. When the English imposed their rule on Ireland in the late sixteenth century, they made their Reformation-based Anglican Protestantism the official Church of Ireland and imposed penalties known as the Penal Laws upon all "dissenters" who refused to accept it. The Scots settlers who came in the thousands brought with them a dissenting Presbyterianism that rapidly took root in the northeastern counties. They suffered religious discrimination under the Penal Laws along with the vast Catholic majority, but they suffered apart, for the barrier of religion discouraged intermarriage, assimilation, or common cause between Catholic and Presbyterian.

Presbyterianism in Ulster was nurtured by ministers educated in the universities of Scotland who moved freely and frequently across the water, creating a common religious tradition. One shared religious practice later taken to America was the evolution of sacramental festivals or holy fairs, which began at Six Mile Water in 1625 and quickly spread throughout Ulster and the southwestern Lowlands. Such fairs were part of a growing attraction to the experience of a personal conversion as a sign of salvation. Lasting several days, the fairs consisted of large crowds of people meeting in open fields and addressed by numerous popular ministers. Hellfire-and-brimstone sermons, prayer vigils, conversions, and confirmations of earlier conversions all evoked intense emotional responses, including screaming, crying, and sometimes fainting spells. The fair culminated in a mass celebration of holy communion by tables full of communicants.

Despite many shared religious practices, Presbyterianism in Ireland took on new and distinct qualities of its own. Unlike their Scottish brethren, who won recognition as the established church of Scotland in 1690, Ulster Presbyterians remained a persecuted minority, distrusted by those Anglicans who governed Ireland. The native Catholics likewise hated them. As a consequence, they developed a defensive and intolerant outlook, called by some a "siege mentality." Their belief that they were surrounded and subject to constant danger of attack was powerfully confirmed by several Catholic rebellions in the seventeenth century.

The Presbyterian community in Ulster experienced persecution and was never, unlike its Scottish counterpart, part of the established church. Fearful, disillusioned by continuing government repression, always having to fight for survival, it developed a determination neither to compromise nor to yield. Ulster Presbyterianism depended for survival not on power and a privileged position but upon the strength and determination of its local parishes and presbyteries, each with its own understanding of Calvinist doctrine. There was less discipline and authority within Irish Presbyterianism, and more independence and diversity, than in the Scottish church. In sum, the Presbyterianism that the Ulster Scots eventually brought to America was characterized by a democratic spirit and was accustomed to entertaining a variety of opinions within the framework of Calvinist belief.

The tens of thousands of Scots who had sought happier circumstances through migration to Ulster had been reshaped and made into a new community in a new land. But many were to prove their willingness to submit to that migratory experience yet again. This time it was a far more permanent and less familiar move three thousand miles across a dark and mighty ocean to the wilderness of North America.

2

Migration from Ulster

One of the features distinguishing the Scotch-Irish as a people was their willingness, perhaps even eagerness, to seek happier circumstances through migration. Their diaspora began in the seventeenth century with the movement of tens of thousands of Scots across the North Channel of the Irish Sea to Ulster. But when their circumstances there soured, they proved willing to pack up again and move to a land they had never seen and knew only by reputation. Once in America they continued to display a readiness to move again and again, predominantly south and west from the main port of entry at Philadelphia, into the mountain frontiers of the new land. The families and individuals who made the move into the southern mountains were, in most cases, the third or fourth generation from the original settlers from Scotland. Willingness to move was becoming part of Scotch-Irish culture.

The plantation experience had created in Ulster a society in which a small landholding elite enjoyed economic and political supremacy over a large body of tenants and laborers. This prevailing landlord-tenant-laborer social structure was common throughout Britain and Europe in the seventeenth and eighteenth centuries. However, three distinctive factors further alienated rural Ulster Scots: they were a persecuted religious minority; they lived and labored not only under landlords but also in a colonial economic situation subject to British rules and restrictions; and the experience of migration was still fresh enough so that their roots in Ulster were not yet deeply planted.

The new settlers had expected a better life than they had left behind in Scotland, and there is every reason to conclude that the expectations of many were met, at least for a time. But the eighteenth century brought vast changes to Ulster society. A rapidly expanding population, increasing scarcity of land, economic change, and religious grievances combined to alter the conditions of life. Throughout Europe, rural people endured hard and hopeless lives with passivity. Unlike most such people experiencing deprivation and misery, and silently nursing their discontent and desire for change, the Ulster Scots saw the prospect of life in another new and better land.

Very few written descriptions of domestic life in eighteenth-century Ulster have survived. One valuable source is a series of prints by William Hincks that illustrates the Irish linen industry in 1783. Though somewhat idealized, this illustration of spinning, reeling, and boiling of yarn reveals much detail. The hearth was the focus of family life and was simply furnished with a few cooking implements such as pot and hook, griddle, and forks. Furniture consisted of a few chairs, a shelf or chest that contained eating implements such as platters, a few spoons and forks, a knife, and a noggin or two for liquids. A salt box hangs near the hearth. Engraving by William Hincks from the Library of Congress Prints and Photographs Division (LC-USZ62-4801), Washington, D.C.

Religious Grievances

It is undoubtedly true that some Ulster settlers cared little about religion, and it is equally true that religion was rarely the only motive for emigration. Yet for Ulster Scots, Presbyterianism remained an essential cultural marker that sharply distinguished them from ruling Anglicans and hostile Gaelic Irish, a source of group strength and, in the eighteenth century, a growing source of grievances. While the British government was committed to the supremacy of Protestantism in Ireland and depended heavily upon Presbyterian support, it was Anglican Protestantism, the religion of the ruling elite, that the government nurtured and protected. While not as severely persecuted as the Catholic majority, Presbyterians were subject to a series of Penal Laws that excluded them from any role in government or the professions. The very operation of their churches was at the mercy of the government. In addition, all Irish were required to pay tithes to the Church of Ireland. While the Penal Laws were not always enforced against Presbyterians, they aroused discontent and often unified the Presbyterian community across class lines.

The principles of Calvinism with their emphasis on human equality and individualism in religious matters also contributed to the growth of radical attitudes and behavior among the Ulster Scot population. Government authorities and landlords repeatedly complained of the role of the Presbyterian ministry in fomenting discontent and a desire to emigrate. By 1750 the land agents who managed the estates of Ulster were expressing increasing dissatisfaction with Presbyterian tenants, whom they regarded as troublesome, defiant, and likely to be involved in the growing movement of agrarian dissent and resistance. Agents often expressed preference for more docile and obedient Catholic tenants.

Clergymen were frequently accused of fomenting emigration, as in this March 1729 letter from Judge Ezekiel Stewart at Fort Stewart, County Donegal: "The Presbyterian ministers have taken their share of pains to seduce their poor ignorant hearers, by bellowing from their pulpits against the Landlords and the Clergy, calling them rackers of Rents, and Servers of Tithes, with other reflections of this nature, which they know is pleasing to their people, at the same time telling them that God has appointed a country for them to depart thence, where they will be freed from the bondage of Egypt and go to the land of Canaan, etc." Stewart believed that women also were instigators: "I can assure your Lordship the women are a great cause of many of our people leaving the kingdom, the accounts the masters of ships and their confederates bring from New England, etc., are so very agreeable to the women that they listen to them with great attention, & every body knows that they have often been thought very proper engines to work upon, & very sensible, in carrying a point where they themselves expect to be the gainers, by the bargain, the masters of ships as I have said before, tell the women they are much more desirable there than the natives of the country, because they are much better housewives and the like, that the men there use their wives like gentlewomen, this makes the women that have daughters to marry to prevail with their Husbands to go thither in hopes of making them Gentlewomen, and those women that have no daughters are in hopes of getting rid of their husbands and getting better ones."—Public Record Office, Northern Ireland

---

Religious grievances, therefore, did make Ulster a less attractive destination for Scottish Presbyterians in the eighteenth century and, in the minds of many already there, a less congenial place to stay. While religious motives did not predominate in the decision to emigrate, they certainly played a part. There are even a few recorded cases of entire congregations emigrating, such as the 467 families led by the Reverend William Martin from Ballymoney, County Antrim, to South Carolina in 1772.

Economic Grievances

Though members of the Ballymoney congregation departed under the leadership of their minister, the surviving traditions of their passage to America reflect their desperate economic circumstances, especially their rapacious treatment at the hands of their landlord. It was above all economic motives—rising rents, low prices for goods, low wages, and periods of crop failure—that drove the Ulster Presbyterians out in waves between 1717 and the end of the century.

At the heart of this economic discontent was growing competition for land and consequent rising rents. The ownership of land rested in the hands of a small privileged class, and the majority of the population either rented from those owners as tenants or worked someone else's land as laborers. It was not only native Catholics who found themselves landless but also most Ulster Scots as well. The social and economic conditions of Ulster made it virtually impossible for tenants and laborers to buy land, and as the population grew throughout the eighteenth century the demand for land pushed rents ever higher. A natural increase in population from a rising birth rate was very pronounced after about 1750, and in some areas of Ulster rents quintupled by the 1770s. However, growing competition for land was evident from the beginning of the century. Scottish migration was at its greatest in the 1690s as Scotland suffered a major famine in the Borders region, and as many as forty thousand emigrants crossed the North Channel to Ulster. At the same time, the Irish government increasingly allowed Catholics to lease land as tenants, creating new competition with the rising Protestant population for land.

The nature of leases also threatened the status of tenants. A large proportion of lands were leased for three lives, but many were let for only twenty-one or thirty-one years. Short leases favored tenants when land was plentiful, but as competition for the land increased, landlords were able to "auction off" leases to the highest bidders. That practice, known as "rack renting," forced renters to bid more than they could afford to pay. The first great wave of American emigration occurred in 1717–1720 and 1725–1727 when leases granted in the 1690s in the Bann Valley in the west of Ulster expired and rents were sharply increased.

The minister's blessing upon a group of departing emigrants. Congregations on occasion migrated as a body, but most emigrants from Ulster sailed to America as individuals or in family groups. Engraving from *Illustrated London News.*

Edmond Kaine, an estate manager in County Monaghan, described the severe economic conditions that accompanied the first wave of emigration in 1720–1722: "money was never worse to get since I came here this 24 years than it is at this time for our market is all down. I know not the meaning of it, but it is believed here that it is occasioned by the hardship England is putting upon us. . . . The tenants have sold their grain and they can get no money when they have delivered it, but I hope the spring will bring better markets or we will be broke altogether. We have had the saddest robbing in the country that ever was known and not only robbing but murdering, killing almost everywhere, where they rob. This is all occasioned by the scarceness of money."—Public Record Office Northern Ireland

"We have had three bad harvests together. . . . Above 4,200 men, women and children have been shipped off from home . . . above 3,100 this last summer. . . . The humour has spread like a contagious distemper, and the people will hardly hear anybody that tries to cure them of their madness. The worse is, that it affects only Protestants, and reigns chiefly in the North, which is the seat of our linen manufacturer." (Letter of Hugh Boulter, lord primate of Ireland, March 1728)— Public Record Office Northern Ireland

---

The economic distress of Ulster tenants was heightened because the British government treated Ireland like a colony. Just as was the case with America, the government was determined to prevent Irish competition with British merchants and farmers. A series of laws forbade Ireland from exporting to Britain any livestock or livestock products except wool, which the English woolen industry demanded in great quantities. Nor was Ireland allowed to export its wool to any other country except Britain. Even its trade with the American colonies was tightly restricted. These colonial restrictions help explain why prices obtained for agricultural products in Ulster lagged far behind rising rents. Only Ireland's linen industry and trade were freely encouraged by the British government. The cultivation of flax became an increasingly important part of the rural economy, for it offered profits twice those of other crops. Thousands of families combined spinning, weaving, and farming, and for them it was the profits of linen that actually paid the rent on their lands. About half of Ireland's exports throughout the eighteenth century consisted of linen. This forced dependence upon one commodity produced employment and profit, but the linen trade was also subject to painful cycles of boom and bust. During the frequent periods of depression many Ulstermen were thrown into desperation, unable to pay their high rents or find other work.

Ironically, those conditions of rents, prices, and the fluctuations of the linen market combined to drive the more prosperous tenant farmers to emigrate to America. The poorer laboring classes that paid no rent but lived by their wages responded to a different crisis. Life became insupportable for the landless poor when bad weather produced crop failure. Poor crops meant high food prices, unemployment, and often famine. The backward agriculture of Ulster was vulnerable to times of crisis, and each occurrence sent thousands of poor, who might have suffered and died quietly in other times and places, seeking new homes. Ulster in the eighteenth century seemed far removed from the promised land it had appeared to be in the seventeenth century. No sooner had the new society taken shape in the north of Ireland than a strong sense of disillusionment took root, particularly during periods of economic depression, and many began to listen to talk of a life and a future elsewhere.

The Lure of America

To seventeenth-century Scots, America had seemed distant and forbidding, while Ireland was near and familiar. But in the century after the Ulster Plantation, the American colonies became a magnet for migration. As part of the British Empire before the Revolution, they offered no barriers of either language or emigration restrictions to Ulster Scots. In addition, the linen trade had established an overseas trade route between the ports of Ireland and American ports on the Delaware River, Philadelphia in particular. Shipowners and sea captains who hauled hundreds of tons of flaxseed annually from Pennsylvania to Ulster were eager for a paying cargo for the return voyage, and they actively encouraged emigration as a solution to Ulster's economic and religious problems. The American colonies suffered from a severe shortage of labor, and their demand for indentured laborers willing to serve for four to seven years in return for passage money encouraged many Irish to migrate. In addition, several colonies feared that their white populations were being dangerously outnumbered by Indians and African slaves. South Carolina on two occasions in the 1730s and 1760s offered land, tools, and seed to whites who would settle within its borders. At those times Charleston rivaled Philadelphia as a port of entry for Ulster immigrants.

The greatest inducement that America offered, which made it seem to be indeed "the best poor man's country," was its promise of cheap land without landlords, tithes, or Penal Laws. To the Irish tenant, rack-rented by his landlord and taxed by a hostile church, America seemed to be the promised land. Letters from sea captains, from land promoters, and from those who had already emigrated to America sang the praises of the New World. To those

Irishmen despairing of their lives in Ulster, America offered a new beginning. Just as Ulster had held out promise for Scots in the seventeenth century, now America lured their "Scotch-Irish" descendants.

The migration began in the 1680s as trade between Ireland and America expanded. This early migration was small, perhaps no more than a few thousand, but it began to surge in 1717. Recent research confirms that substantial numbers of Catholics and even some Anglicans migrated. But the majority of the Irish emigrants to America between 1717 and 1800 were Presbyterians from Ulster. Five Ulster ports—Londonderry, Portrush, Larne, Belfast, and Newry—dominated the emigrant trade, although significant numbers did leave from southern ports such as Cork, Drogheda, Dublin, Sligo, and Waterford. Agents hired by shipowners, American land speculators, and those seeking to profit from indentured labor scoured the Ulster countryside promoting the prospects for poor men in America. Advertisements and letters and testimonials from those gone on ahead were used to stimulate interest and appeared frequently in the Belfast *News Letter* and the *Londonderry Journal*. For those too poor to afford passage, contracting as an indentured servant in America offered an opportunity that a majority of the migrants had no choice but to accept. While some clusters of parishioners or villagers were led by ministers or land developers, in general Ulster migration in the eighteenth century was a family undertaking.

Interest in migration rose and fell in marked linkage with economic conditions. The years of the American Revolution, of course, curtailed that migration as wartime conditions made travel across the Atlantic virtually impossible. With the conclusion of the war, migration resumed. In all, some 250,000 people left for America between 1717 and 1800. According to a recent estimate, 20,000 were Anglo-Irish, 20,000 Gaelic Irish, and the remainder Ulster Scots or Scotch-Irish, as they came to be called in America. Despite government concern that this migration would weaken Protestant rule in Ireland, the authorities failed to take action to restrict it until after the alarmingly heavy flow of people left in the 1770s.

In April 1773 the Londonderry Journal *expressed alarm at the high rate of emigration, estimating that some 17,500 persons had sailed to America from Ulster ports since 1771: "The great part of these Emigrants paid their passage, which at 3 pounds 10 shillings each amounted to 60,725 pounds, most of them people employed in the Linen Manufacture, or Farmers, and of some property which they turned into money and carried with them.*

FOR THE FLOURISHING CITIES OF

Philadelphia and New-York,

THE remarkable faft failing Brig FRIEND-SHIP of NEWRY, burthen 200 Tons, with a New Medditerranean Pafs, WILLIAM FORREST Mafter ; will be clear to fail for the above Ports the firft of May next.—She is roomy between the Decks, and as no more Paffengers will be taken than can be comfortably accommodated, thofe who wifh to embrace fo favourable an opportunity, are requefted to apply immediately to Mr. George Woodhoufe, Portadown ; Mr. Sam. Murphy, or Mr. John Carr, Rathfriland ; the Owner Anthony Hill, Ship-wright, Warren-Point ; or the Captain on Board. And as the faid Brig is deftined annually for the trade of carrying Paffengers, it will be a further inducement for her Owner to do all that lies in his power to make the paffage comfortable.

Newry, 20th March, **1792.**

Advertisements such as this one appeared regularly in the newspapers of Belfast and Londonderry as shipowners and captains promoted emigration for profit. Advertisement from Belfast *News Letter*, 1792.

. . . This removal is sensibly felt in this country—This prevalent humour of industrious Protestants withdrawing from this once flourishing corner of the kingdom, seems to be increasing; and it is thought the number will be considerably larger this year than ever.

"The North of Ireland has been occasionally used to emigration, for which the American settlements have been much beholden:—But till now, it was chiefly the very meanest of the people who went off, mostly in the station of indented servants and such as had become obnoxious to their mother country. In short, it is computed from many concurrent circumstances, that the North of Ireland has in the last five or six years been drained of one fourth of its trading class, and the like proportion of the manufacturing people—Where the evil will end, remains only in the womb of time to determine."

"The death of our landlord, and others coming in and raising the rents, prevented my mother from giving her children more than a very limited education. This together with the

many difficulties we laboured under in Ireland, induced a wish on my part, to try my fortune in some other part of the world. I accordingly in the 28th year of my age, obtained her consent to come to America for the purpose of procuring the necessary means of bringing herself and family to this land of liberty, where we would no longer feel the oppression of haughty landlords, and where virtue and good conduct give a passport to the highest stations of society."—Portion of a letter from James Patton (one of the first residents of Asheville, North Carolina) to his children, describing why he departed his home in County Derry in 1783 (Racine, Wisconsin, 1845)

The Atlantic Passage

Once the decision to emigrate had been made, the prospective settler placed himself and his family at the mercy of the sea and the sea captain. Sailing across the Atlantic in the eighteenth century was a hazardous and frightening experience. It lasted from six to ten weeks and involved the danger of violent storms, disease, pirates, shortages of food and water, and the lack of concern

Very few emigrant ships from Ulster were lost at sea during the eighteenth century—only three are recorded—but many emigrants experienced the terror of a violent storm, in which people might be lost overboard. Engraving from *Illustrated London News.*

or even brutality of the captains. As "the cheaper the cost of the voyage, the greater the profits," captains and shipowners were encouraged to crowd as many people as possible between decks less than five feet apart and inadequately lit and ventilated by portholes. When that overcrowding was finally addressed by a law in 1828, the lawmakers saw fit to require only 20½ square inches of open deck space per passenger. Profits could also be increased by skimping on food, which typically consisted of bread, potatoes, and sometimes salted beef.

"Saturday 7th. Last night was most tremendous all the night. At 11 o'clock the vessel shipped a sea which washed away the lee quarter boom, boards . . . and filled the cabin full of water; which alarmed every soul aboard. We expected every moment would be the last—in short, words cannot relate what we felt on the occasion as its happening at night made it still more terrible. I believe if the vessel had gone to the bottom I could not have stirred out of my berth. The gale somewhat abated this morning but still a very high sea running and some spray flying over the vessel. . . . Mr. Neil's two youngest children and the sailor before mentioned all bad in the smallpox."—Journal of John Cunningham, a passenger aboard the ship America, *describing his voyage from Belfast to Boston, September 27 to December 12, 1795, Public Record Office Northern Ireland*

Fortunate passengers traveling in uncrowded ships had the opportunity to examine maps of the new country that would be their home. Engraving from *Illustrated London News.*

Delaware Bay, July 4th, 1771.

Meſſeurs Henry and Robert Joy,

You will confer a ſingular Obligation on thoſe of your Country-men that went as Paſſengers to Philadelphia in America, from Bel-faſt, laſt May, by giving the following a Place in your uſeful Paper.

WE think that we would deſervedly incur the Cenſure of the Judicious and Impartial, ſhould we omit thus publickly mentioning, the Conduct of our Captain, Mr. James Malcom, whoſe every Action was calculated for the Advantage, Convenience and Pleaſure of his Paſſengers. With a Liberality not generally practiſed, he diſtributed a greater Variety of Proviſions than was promiſed; which, with his humane Uſage, helped much to the rendering the Voyage unhurtful and agreeable.

The Friends of the Paſſengers, ſome of whom, by a Diverſity of Accidents, may hear no Account for a conſiderable Time, will, we believe, be glad to know that we all arrived, vigorous and healthy.

From no other Motive than a grateful Acknowledgement of the Captain's kind, ſocial, benevolent and friendly Behaviour, do we whoſe Names are underwritten deſire this to be made public; and, that thoſe of our Friends who deſign to become Adventurers to this Land of Milk and Honey, may know where to find a Man who is particularly adapted for the Trade in which he is employed

By exerting every Endeavour, and watching every Opportunity that could render a Voyage healthful, ſhort and pleaſant, has he drawn the above Character from us; from which we hope his future Paſ-ſengers will have no reaſon to diſſent.

John Mc. Cullough	John Mc. Clughan	Hugh Ramſey
Thos. Alexander	Samuel Irwin	Samuel Colvin
James Mc. Henry	John Storry	Robert Bell
Michael Rankin	Richard Mc. Quon	Wm. Meek
Francis Lee	James Campbell	David Fairſervice
James Boyd	John Hill	Wm. Patterſon
Adam Johnſton	Thos. Hill	David Parkinſon
Wm. Thompſon	Samuel Long	Hans Woods
Daniel Young	James Duncan	John Cairns
John Gallaway	Samuel Duff	John Cooper
James Laird	David Leathin	John Clark
Wm. Watſon	Wm. Hallyday	James Laird
Matthew Mc. Cauley	Robert Corry	Samuel Allan
Hugh O'Quin	Alex. Boyle	George Williſon
Joſeph Wilſon	Henry Hannah	
Hamilton Potts	Wm. Stirling	

Letters such as this one, written by emigrants from their new home in America to endorse their ship captains and to encourage others to migrate, were often published in Ulster newspapers. They were also a way of letting relatives know they had arrived safely. Letter from Belfast *News Letter*, 1771.

From the Port of Larne

#	Ship	Captain	Tonnage	Destination	Time of Sailing	Freight	No. of Souls
1	Jupiter	John Allen	250	Charlestown	July 1771		
2	James & Mary	J. Workman	200	New York	Oct: 71		
3	Jupiter	R. Shutter	250	Charlestown	Ap: 72		
4	James & Mary	J. Workman	200	Ditto	Ap: 72		
5	Betty	A. Woodside	250	Ditto	Aug: 72		
6	James & Mary	J. Workman	200	Ditto	Aug: 72		
7	Lord Dunluce	Jas. Gillis	400	Ditto	Sep: 72		
			1750				

From the Port of Belfast

#	Ship	Captain	Tonnage	Destination	Time of Sailing	Freight	No. of Souls
1	Polly	Dd. McCutcheon	200	Philadelphia	Mar. 71	80	80
2	Philadelphia	Jas. Malcolm	250	Ditto	Apr. 71	251	300
3	Prince of Wales	C. McKenzie	250	New York	Apr. 71		60
4	Kitty & Peggy	D. Ferguson	300	Philadelphia	May 71	228	270
5	Polly	Dd. McCutcheon	200	Ditto	Aug: 71	130	150
6	Hopewell	J: Ash	250	Charlestown	Oct: 71	220	260
7	Brittania	J. Clendenen	300	Savannah	Oct: 71	300	350
8	Friendship	W: McCulloch	250	Philadelphia	Mar. 72	236	250
9	Prince of Wales	C. McKenzie	400	Ditto	Apr. 72	327	390
10	Philadelphia	Jas. Malcolm	250	Ditto	May 72	242	287
11	Will & John	Jno. Baker	150	St. Johns Gulf St. Lawrence	May 72	106	106
12	Brittania	Jas. Clendenen	300	Charlestown	Oct: 72	84	105
13	Friendship	W. McCulloch	250	Philadelphia	Aug: 72	69	76
14	Elizabeth	Dd. Brown	250	Savannah	Oct: 72	197	240
15	Hopewell	Tho: Ash	250	Charlestown	Sep: 72	210	245
16	Pensilva. Farmer	C. Robinson	350	Ditto	Oct: 72	176	230
17	Friendship	W. McCulloch	250	Ditto	Mar: 73	248	280
			4450			3164	3679

From the Port of Newry

#	Ship	Captain	Tonnage	Destination	Time of Sailing	Freight	No. of Souls
1	Newry Pachet	C. Robison	300	Philadelphia	Apr: 71		
2	Pensilva. Farmer	R. Johnston	350	Ditto	Mar: 71		
3	Betsy	Ger. Brown	300	Balt. & Charlestown	Mar: 71		
4	Dolphin	T. Finlay	300	Philadelphia	Mar: 71		
5	Jenny & Polly	D. Lawrence	300	Baltimore	May 71		
6	Venus	Jno. Lloyd	250	Anapolis	July 71		
7	New York	Mos. Rankin	400	New York	July 71		
8	Robert	Mo. Russell	300	Ditto	Sep: 71		
9	Newry assist.	Jas. Chevers	300	Philadelphia	Sep: 71		
10	Robert	M. Russell	300	New York	Ap: 72		
11	Pheby & Peggy	Dd. McCulloch	350	Philadelphia	June 72		
12	Nedham	W. Chevers	400	Newcastle & Philad.	Sep: 72		
13	Freemason	J. Semple	250	Charlestown	Oct: 72		
14	Newry assistance	R. Cunningham	300	New Cast. & Philad.	Aug: 72		

This listing of emigrant ship departures from Ulster ports between 1771 and 1773 was compiled by Robert Stephenson, an inspector for the Irish Linen Board. Stephenson was concerned about the impact of emigration on the linen industry. The columns indicate the names of ships, captains, ship tonnages, destination, dates of departure, freight tonnages, and numbers of passengers.

If the passenger survived all of this (and most did), then one further obstacle lay in wait for those who had been unable to pay for their passage and had not signed indentures with an American employer. Their arrival in an American port meant a further wait aboard ship, often with little food or water and threatened by disease. These "redemptioners" were not allowed to disembark until the captain had sold their labor to redeem the cost of their passage. Only when an employer had paid the captain for their fare could they join their fellow passengers in setting foot on what they hoped would be their promised land.

3

Pennsylvania: A First American Home

T he ports of the Delaware River were not the only destination for the shiploads of Ulster immigrants in the eighteenth century. The first arrivals came to the New England states, which had been settled earlier by English Calvinists. The migrants were almost immediately pushed to the frontier by a scarcity of good land and by a cold reception from colonial authorities and residents of small farm communities, who regarded the Scotch-Irish poor with distrust. New York received from 15 to 25 percent of the immigrant ships arriving from Ulster ports, though there too colonial land policies and enforcement of the established church served to dampen Presbyterian enthusiasm for settlement. Bounties offered by the South Carolina legislature attracted thousands of settlers in the 1730s and 1760s. But the preeminent destination for Ulster immigrants throughout the eighteenth century was the colony of Pennsylvania, with its broad policy of religious toleration, its hunger for indentured labor, its rich lands, and its strong commercial ties with Ulster. Even as land became more scarce and expensive after 1750, other factors preserved Pennsylvania's preeminence, not the least of which was the established Scotch-Irish community that created a network of family and friends to draw the new emigrants across the Atlantic and offer them support and encouragement.

————————

James Logan, provincial secretary of Pennsylvania, was an early advocate of Ulster immigration. In 1720, concerned about increased Indian disturbances on Pennsylvania's frontier, he wrote: "I therefore thought it might be prudent to plant a settlement of such men as those who formerly had so bravely defended Londonderry and Inniskillen as a frontier in case of any disturbances. . . . These people if kindly used will be ordered as they have hitherto been and easily dealt with. They will also, I expect, be a leading example to others." Nine years later, Logan's outlook had changed dramatically: "A settlement of five families from the North of Ireland gives me more trouble than fifty of any other people. . . . It looks as if Ireland is to send all her inhabitants hither. . . . The common fear is, that if they continue to come, they will make themselves proprietors of the province."

After they arrived in Philadelphia and were freed from whatever indentures some might have entered into, the immigrants were ready to look for a new life of their own. The colony of Pennsylvania had a growing commercial economy and town life, and it offered a variety of occupations to new settlers. For most, however, life in America meant a life upon the land. Several factors affected Scotch-Irish settlement in Pennsylvania. For those who came early, the prospects did indeed give the colony the appearance of a promised land. The soil itself, particularly the limestone soils north and west of Philadelphia, was extremely fertile. It was not too heavily forested, and it was populated by abundant game. The climate, while colder than Ulster in winter

Long weeks at sea culminated in arrival in Philadelphia, colonial America's largest city. There the fortunate immigrant was greeted by family or friends. More frequently, the individual would meet for the first time the merchant or farmer who had purchased his or her indenture. Engraving from Edwin Tunis, *Colonial Living* (Cleveland and New York: World Publishing Company, 1957), frontispiece.

and hotter in summer, was as generous as the land. In the early decades of the century, land was cheap and plentiful. By 1730 the population had begun to explode, and by 1740 most of the rich lands around Philadelphia had been occupied. Scotch-Irish settlement in Pennsylvania was shaped by the fact that the vast majority came after the land near Philadelphia had been claimed and prices had risen. Thus the Scotch-Irish moved westward, filling Chester and Lancaster counties and crossing the Susquehanna River into York County.

"Land [in Pennsylvania] is of all Prices. Even from ten Pounds, to one hundred Pounds a hundred, according to the goodness or else the situation thereof, & Grows dearer every year by Reason of Vast Quantities of People that come here yearly from Several Parts of the world, therefore thee and thy family or any that I wish well I would desire to make what Speed you can to come here the Sooner the Better.

"This county yields Extraordinary Increase of all sorts of Grain likewise . . . so that it is as Plentiful a County as any can be if people will be Industrious. . . . All sorts of Provisions are Extraordinary Plenty in Philadelphia market where County people bring in their commodities.

"This county abounds in fruit, Scarce an house but has an Apple, Peach & Cherry orchard, as for Chestnuts, Walnuts, and Hazel nuts, Strawberries, Billberrys and Mullberrys they grow wild in the woods and fields in vast Quantities."—Robert Parke, a Pennsylvania Quaker, to his sister in Ireland, 1725, Public Record Office Northern Ireland

---

Ethnicity and Adaptation

Most settlers in southeastern Pennsylvania seem to have built houses near their kith and kin. But while the Scotch-Irish tended to seek one another out as they settled and were not keen on living among Germans, whose language they did not understand, they did not create large ethnic communities. Such was not their inclination, nor did they have much choice in the matter. A variety of European peoples had preceded them, and especially in areas such as the Lancaster Plain, they found themselves living among a rich mixture of ethnic groups: English, French Huguenots, Germans, Welsh, Swedes, as well as Delaware and Conestoga Indians. The Scotch-Irish from the earliest time of

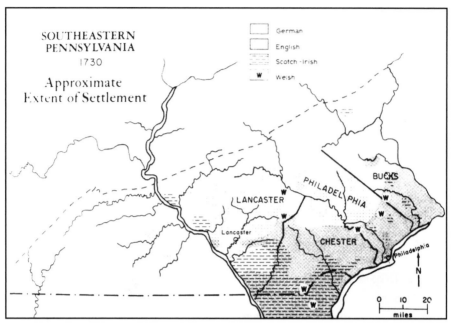

Newly arrived Ulster immigrants found themselves among a rich variety of ethnic groups that had come before them to southeastern Pennsylvania. Map from James T. Lemon, *The Best Poor Man's Country* (Baltimore: Johns Hopkins University Press, 1972), 49.

their American experience mixed with a wide variety of ethnic traditions, from which they quickly adopted many practices.

One of the difficulties of studying the history of the Scotch-Irish in America is the problem of identifying ethnic boundaries, of deciding what is uniquely Scotch-Irish so that they can be identified as a distinct group. Most scholars agree that in terms of material culture, it is much more difficult to isolate a "Scotch-Irish style" than a German or English style in the arts or crafts, in dress, or in architecture. The essence of the Scotch-Irish style is simplicity and practicality. The settlers from Ulster were a people whose life was made simple by their poverty. They were a people practiced in abandoning their past, for twice in living memory they had moved. In the sixteenth century they had rejected a religion rich in style and tradition for an austere Calvinism that scorned outward appearances and emphasized the private and individual. The result of all this was the extraordinary willingness of the Scotch-Irish to learn from and adopt the ways of others at the expense of their own culture and traditions. Scotch-Irish traits must be looked for less in terms of material culture and more in terms of nonmaterial traits, in attitudes and behavioral features such as willingness to adapt, mobility, attachment to Presbyterianism, and land-use practices.

Frontier life was often a shock to those not accustomed to it: "We dined on fish—suckers and chubbs and on venison. It is a level, rich, pleasant spot, the broad creek running by the door. . . . Soon after we dined two Indian boys bolted in (they never knock or speak at the door) with seven large fish, one would weigh two pounds. . . . Down they sat in the ashes before the fire, stirred up the coals and laid on their flesh. . . . When they were gone I sat me down on a three legged stool to write. This house looks and smells like a shambles; raw flesh and blood in every part, mangled wasting flesh on every shelf. Hounds licking up the blood from the floor; an openhearted landlady; naked Indians and children; ten thousand flies; oh! I fear there are as many fleas. . . . Seize me soon kind sleep, lock me in thy sweet embrace. . . . For all this settlement I would not live here for two such settlements; not for five hundred a year."—A description of a homestead in central Pennsylvania, 1775, written by an itinerant clergyman and quoted in Robert Secor, gen. ed., Pennsylvania 1776 *(University Park: Pennsylvania State University, 1976)*

The Scotch-Irish brought a history of intercultural relations with them when they arrived in America. In Ulster they had found themselves cheek-by-jowl with English settlers and the native Irish, who, although historically sharing many customs with them, still preserved a strongly independent identity and distinctive culture. Despite differences of religion and official efforts to segregate the native Irish, some cultural blending occurred. It was in America, however, that the Scotch-Irish capacity for cultural adaptation fully manifested itself.

Examples of Scotch-Irish adaptation are found in all areas of their lives. In agriculture, the shift from oats, barley, sheep, and cattle to an economy that relied heavily upon wheat, corn, and pigs occurred partly in response to a new environment but also from contacts with Indian and other European farmers. The dwellings of the Scotch-Irish also changed in America, because the log cabin with which they have been historically associated they in fact copied from Swedes and Germans, although they retained the floor plan of the Ulster

Ulster immigrants brought their traditional skills for transforming the coarse fibers of flax into linen. Though the making of linen ceased to be an industry in the American colonies, it long remained a part of domestic life. In this engraving by William Hincks, scutching and hackling the flax are depicted. Engraving from the Library of Congress (LC-USZ62-14838), Washington, D.C.

stone cottage. Other examples of cultural borrowing are the dulcimer and the long rifle, which have come to be strongly identified as Scotch-Irish but in fact were adopted from the Pennsylvania German community. The Scotch-Irish borrowed wherever they found themselves among new peoples, but especially in southeastern Pennsylvania, where the diversity of ethnic groups was so great and where ethnic settlements were so strongly contiguous.

The experiences of James Patton, a young weaver from County Derry who spent six years in Pennsylvania following his arrival in 1783, illustrate the opportunities and difficulties that awaited the Scotch-Irish. Patton, who described his immigrant life in a letter to his children when he was eighty-four years old, left Ulster because of increased rents and his overwhelming desire to escape "the oppressions of haughty landlords." His immediate goal in Pennsylvania was to save enough money to bring his family across. Although he was a weaver by trade, he first found work as an agricultural laborer, clearing other people's land. The work was unfamiliar and difficult, and he injured himself. He was able to find short periods of employment as a weaver, but the work did not last.

Faced with more heavy manual labor—digging wells, clearing land, and blowing up rock—and long periods of illness, Patton was overtaken as many immigrants must have been with loneliness, depression, and bouts of tears. But, like others, he benefited from the network of Ulstermen who had come before him, seeking advice, comfort, and friendship among his compatriots, whom he always referred to as "Irishmen." He worked and lived with members of other ethnic groups too, especially English Quakers and Germans, whom he called "Dutchmen," who also taught him a great deal about his new homeland and, in particular, about the possibilities of trade. Unlike most Scotch-Irish in America, Patton did not become a farmer. Instead he made his fortune as a merchant carrying dry goods southward along the Great Wagon Road and as a cattle drover bringing herds north from the Carolinas to Philadelphia. In that way he traveled to the mountains of North Carolina, where he eventually became a leading figure in the frontier town of Asheville.

Depression and fear of failure were the frequent companions of many newly arrived immigrants: "I had boarded some time with a Mr. Shaw, a countryman of mine, and when I left his house, he took two horses and assisted me along the road for some distance. He inquired where I was going? I told him I was going to Canada, that my mother had told me, she had an uncle and brother in that country, who had become rich; and that I would endeavor to find them out. But this was not my real motive, I was really afraid that nothing awaited me but misery and poverty, and that news would reach Ireland that I was in a most destitute situation, and being naturally of a proud spirit, I wished to go where I should not be known by any person. My health was at this time so bad, that I was unable to do anything for myself; but thanks to the great and mighty God! I had a mind that enabled me to surmount all difficulties. When Mr. Shaw left me, I went off the road into the woods sat down by an oak tree, and gave vent to a torrent of tears."—Letter of James Patton, describing his early life in Pennsylvania

---

Mobility and the Land

The goal of most immigrants was to obtain land, but for the Scotch-Irish, at least, not necessarily to own it. A common grievance raised against them by colonial authorities was their habit of squatting on land and not bothering to claim it officially and pay for it. That habit resulted in part from their poverty and in part from the way they used the land. Undoubtedly many did adopt the intensive agriculture suited to the rich lands of Pennsylvania and practiced by their German neighbors. Intensive agriculture placed a high value upon careful cropping and fertilizing, upon efficiency and permanence. Many Scotch-Irish farmers who lacked the skills or the money to farm the best lands adhered to the traditional Ulster ways, which combined cropping with herding and hunting, did not require large amounts of the best soils, and in fact encouraged movement as land and game wore out.

Pennsylvania Presbyterianism

Pennsylvania was a generous land, a first and last home for many immigrants. William Penn, the Quaker founder of the colony, had provided for wide participation in government. Presbyterianism had been brought to nearby Maryland in 1683 by a Scotch-Irishman, Francis Makemie, and the first presbytery in the New World was founded in Philadelphia in 1706. By 1717 there were thirteen organized Presbyterian churches in the area. Many Presbyterian ministers came with the Scotch-Irish into Pennsylvania, but they could not meet the growing demands of new congregations. By the late 1730s the presbyteries of Pennsylvania were receiving requests for ministers from Scotch-Irish communities as far away as the Valley of Virginia. It was obvious that the universities of Scotland could not meet the American need for Presbyterian clergy and that the colonies would have to educate their own. In 1726 the Reverend William Tennant, pastor at Neshaminy in Bucks County, began a "Log College" to teach the disciplines of his church to young men. This first Presbyterian educational effort coincided with the powerful religious revival known as the Great Awakening, a fervent evangelical movement that swept through the middle colonies and inspired the Presbyterian Church with a determination to carry religion to the people. It produced division as well as enthusiasm, for many Presbyterian leaders saw the Great Awakening as a lowering of clerical standards and a threat to traditional Calvinist doctrine. Though the Great Awakening divided the church, it also prepared it to respond to the growing challenge of religion on the southern frontier.

New Horizons Again

Still, southeastern Pennsylvania did not, in fact could not, become the terminus of the Scotch-Irish migration. Ulstermen continued to flood into the colony throughout the eighteenth century, and the pressures of population growth made it impossible for the land to support all who came. By 1760 the Pennsylvania frontier pressed up against the Blue Mountains, where the first ridges of the high Alleghenies and hostile Indians barred westward settlement. By midcentury, many who arrived in Philadelphia passed through without pausing, their eyes on another destination. In addition, some who had obtained land in the Pennsylvania Piedmont decided not to stay. Whether it was because of soil exhaustion caused by their wasteful land-use practices, an antipathy to living in large communities, a search for even cheaper land and a better climate, or some kind of culturally induced "restlessness," significant numbers of Scotch-Irish sold their lands and joined the growing southwestward movement into the Valley of Virginia, which for some would eventually lead to the mountains of western North Carolina.

The Catheys were typical of those Scotch-Irish who once owned land in southeastern Pennsylvania, only to move further south with the expanding frontier. They were descendants of a Scottish family that migrated to Ulster in response to King James's plantation scheme and apparently settled in County Monaghan. Sometimes before 1719 James Cathey came to America, for in that year he is recorded as having sold a piece of land on the Delaware River in Cecil County, Maryland. In 1724 he was residing in Chester County, Pennsylvania, but by 1733 he held a license for 200 acres in Lancaster County. Five years later his son William purchased 466 acres in the Beverly Manor in the Shenandoah Valley. By 1743 James held a patent for 1,350 acres there, as well as 1,000 acres in Orange County, Virginia.

Yet by 1751 the Catheys had left the Shenandoah Valley. James and George appeared in Rowan County, North Carolina, in 1749, having settled west of the Yadkin River in an area known as the "Irish Settlement." James died there in 1757, but other members of his family migrated again and settled about 1798 in what would become the western mountain county of Haywood in North Carolina. The Cathey family illustrates the process of migration along the advancing southern frontier.

Michel Guillaume Jean de Crèvecoeur came from France to the American colonies in 1759. In 1782, while a farmer in Pennsylvania, he wrote Letters from an American Farmer *in praise of life in the new nation. The work included this passage: "Ye poor Europeans, ye who sweat, and work for the great—ye, who are obliged to give so many sheaves to the church, so many to your lords, so many to your governments, and have hardly any left for yourselves—ye, who only breathe the air of nature, because it cannot be withheld from you; it is here that you can conceive the possibility of those feelings I have been describing; it is here the laws of naturalization invite every one to partake of our great labours and felicity, to till unrented, untaxed lands."*

4

The Valley of Virginia and the Carolina Piedmont: The Great Wagon Road

S outheastern Pennsylvania offered a first American home to thousands of Scotch-Irish, although for many it was little more than a port of entry or a temporary home. It was not in the rich soils and growing communities of southeastern Pennsylvania that the Scotch-Irish would play their greatest role but in the backcountry of America—in western New York, across the Alleghenies in western Pennsylvania, and especially down the Great Wagon Road in Virginia and the Carolinas. Ulstermen like James Patton took the lead in building the commercial connections and the small frontier towns, but above all the Scotch-Irish were agricultural pioneers who contributed significantly to the creation of rural frontier society.

As settlers pressed against the Allegheny Mountains in central Pennsylvania, they faced two possible choices. The first was to cross the mountains into western Pennsylvania. The reluctance of Indians to sell their land and their violent reaction to intruders threw most pioneers back upon a second choice: to move southwestward into the Virginia and Carolina backcountry.

English writers frequently expressed their prejudice against the Scotch-Irish. In his Account of the European Settlements in America *(1757), Edmund Burke wrote: "The number of white people in Virginia is . . . growing every day more numerous by the migration of the Irish who, not succeeding so well in Pennsylvania as the more frugal and industrious Germans, sell their lands in that province to the latter, and take up new ground in the remote countries in Virginia, Maryland and South Carolina. These are chiefly Presbyterians from the northern part of Ireland, who in American are generally called Scotch-Irish."*

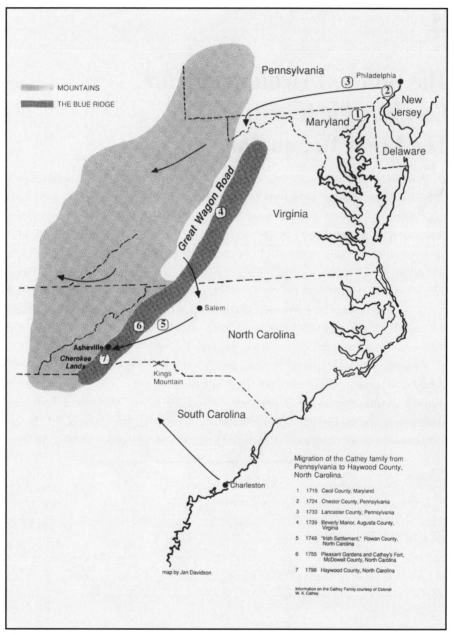

map by Jan Davidson

This map shows the predominant migration routes south and west from Pennsylvania and northwest from Charleston, South Carolina. The experiences of the Cathey family are typical of the generational movement that brought thousands of families to the southern Appalachians. Map by Jan Davidson.

The Great Valley of Virginia

There were good reasons for choosing the southern route. The mouth of the Shenandoah Valley was broad, and it and the larger Valley of Virginia of which it was a part contained gently rolling, fertile land that contrasted sharply with the rough topography of the Alleghenies. Land throughout the entire Valley of Virginia was cheap, and there were no settled Indian populations. The colonial government of Virginia was eager to encourage settlement there to create a buffer against nomadic Indians. Finally, there were no boundary disputes, such as the one over the location of the Pennsylvania-Maryland border, to leave land titles in a state of uncertainty.

Settlement proceeded southward with the better lands in the northern part of the valley, known as the Shenandoah Valley, claimed first. Germans took the lead in occupying the northern end between 1726 and 1730. As had been the case in Pennsylvania, the Scotch-Irish were latecomers. However, a strong surge of Ulster immigration after 1727, combined with Virginia's policy of granting large tracts of land to speculators to spur settlement, drew growing numbers of Ulstermen into western Virginia. Two large tracts were granted to men who specifically sought out Scotch-Irish settlers. In 1736 William Beverly received the 11,491-acre Beverly Manor in what would become Augusta County, and three years later Benjamin Borden was granted 92,100 acres in Rockbridge County. These two tracts in the higher and hillier southern end of the Valley became, after southeastern Pennsylvania, a second home for the Scotch-Irish and contained the heaviest concentration of Ulster settlers in the American colonies. Another James Patton, an Ulster ship captain who traded between the British Isles and the Rappahannock River, settled in the Beverly Manor and was active as an agent organizing direct Ulster migration to western Virginia. As a consequence, the majority of those who came directly from the Old World to Augusta and Rockbridge counties from the 1730s on were Scotch-Irish, as were a significant number of those who came from the farms and towns of southeastern Pennsylvania. Yet even in those two counties, where the Scotch-Irish comprised two-thirds of the white population, the cultural intermixing and borrowing begun in Pennsylvania continued.

But the Valley of Virginia was not just a place to settle. Because of its geographic location it also played an increasingly important role as a route between the middle and southern colonies. Throughout the eighteenth and early nineteenth centuries the commercial and cultural connections of Virginia and Carolina frontier settlements were not east-west to the coastal towns but north-south to the radical politics and Presbyterianism of Pennsylvania. Missionaries first, then traders and cattle drivers, and finally settlers looking for new land, all used the Valley as a highway in ever-growing numbers. Eventually its fame spread far and wide as the route of the Great Wagon Road, from Philadelphia to the Yadkin River valley in North Carolina, some 450 miles in all. Even people who had taken out land grants in the Valley of Virginia joined this southward migration, as movement and change came more and more to characterize the constantly shifting southwestern frontier.

The hope of owning land drove generation after generation of settlers to the westward-moving frontier. The surveyor was a central figure in the process of transferring the ancestral lands of Native Americans to European immigrants. This painting of George Washington as a surveyor entitled *The Young Surveyor* was painted for the Washington National Insurance Company by Walter Haskell Hinton, date unknown.

The motives of settlers in leaving lands they had bought in western Virginia were as many and varied as those who had done the same in Pennsylvania. Undoubtedly an important consideration was profit. Because it was a major migration route, newcomers were constantly passing through. Many preferred to purchase already developed land than to face the hardships of wilderness pioneering. Those who had bought undeveloped land and settled it could usually make a considerable profit by selling it to latecomers. They could then move on to the edge of the frontier, where their profits enabled them to buy larger tracts of cheaper land. In that way family fortunes could be accumulated, and one kind of settler replaced another as the frontier moved south and west.

The Carolina Piedmont

The route that most Scotch-Irish traveled to the Carolinas followed the Valley of Virginia to the Staunton River. There it turned east with the river, passing through the Blue Ridge Mountains. The route then crossed the Dan River into North Carolina and led into the new lands between the Yadkin and Catawba rivers. There many immigrants dispersed to settle, but others continued into the South Carolina Piedmont.

The population of North Carolina grew at a rapid rate in the eighteenth century, from 36,000 in 1730 (primarily in the Coastal Plain) to 70,000 in 1750 and 180,000 by 1770. The most rapid area of growth was the Piedmont backcountry. The population of Rowan County quadrupled between 1754 and 1770 as settlers poured down the Great Wagon Road. A much smaller number of Scotch-Irish entered the region through the port of Charleston.

The attractions of Piedmont North Carolina were many. The price of land was lower than in Pennsylvania or western Virginia, and problems with Indians seemed fewer, especially when compared to the bloody Indian attacks on Augusta County in 1745. Perhaps most important was the image of North Carolina that was created in the minds of Europeans and other colonists—rich soil, abundant game, and limitless opportunity. Arthur Dobbs, a wealthy Ulster landowner, received a large grant of lands in Mecklenburg and Cabarrus counties in North Carolina. From 1754 to 1765 he served as colonial governor of North Carolina and was active in publicizing a favorable view of the colony among Ulstermen. Although he was not personally able to entice many Irishmen directly to his colony, his descriptions of North Carolina, which emphasized good land and

Arthur Dobbs of Castle Dobbs, County Antrim, in Ulster. Dobbs represented Carrickfergus in the Irish Parliament from 1727 to 1730 and served as surveyor general in Ireland in 1730. He was governor of the royal colony of North Carolina from 1754 to 1765.

freedom of conscience, circulated in Ireland and contributed to the positive opinion that was forming there of life in the new land. The Englishman Arthur Young, in his travels in Ireland in the early 1770s, reported that the poor preparing to emigrate talked much of North Carolina.

The central and western parts of North Carolina acquired a favorable reputation as an area for settlement early in the eighteenth century. Explorer John Lawson wrote in 1709: "[Blackwards, near the Mountains, you meet with the richest soil, a sweet, thin Air, dry Roads, pleasant small murmuring Streams, and several beneficial Productions and Species."—Lawson, A New Voyage to Carolina *(London, 1709)*

"It must be owned North Carolina is a Very happy Country where people may live with the least labour that they can in any part of the world, and if the lower parts are moist and consequently a little unwholesome every where above Chowan, as far as I have seen, people may live both in health and plenty. T'is the same I doubt not in the uplands in that Province."—William Byrd II, A History of the Dividing Line betwixt Virginia and North Carolina *(1731)*

*"There is scarce any history, either ancient or modern, which affords an account of such a rapid and sudden increase of inhabitants in a back Frontier country, as that of North Carolina." (*Connecticut Courant, *November 30, 1767)*

The earliest settlers on the creeks and river bottoms west of the Yadkin River appeared in 1746. This time the Scotch-Irish preceded other ethnic groups and obtained the best lands. Of the three settlements that grew up before 1750, the "Irish settlement" at the head of the Second Creek of the South Yadkin River was the largest and was predominantly Scotch-Irish. By 1749 there were some fourteen families in the Irish settlement, led by James and George Cathey. That settlement was possibly the first English-speaking one in North Carolina situated so far from a navigable river. Its church, Thyatira Presbyterian, is the first known house of worship west of the Yadkin. The growth of the community was rapid, with more than one hundred new families, most Scotch-Irish, obtaining land there in the next fifteen years.

"On his return from the expedition [against the Cherokees] he purchased a beautiful spot of land on Crowder's Creek, about four miles from Kings Mountain, in the same county, and removed there in the fall of 1763, being then a fresh part; he cultivated some land and raised stock in abundance and I can then remember that my mother and her assistants made as much butter in one summer as purchased a Negro woman in Charlestown. My father hunted and killed deer in abundance and maintained his family on wild meat in style. I remember he kept me following him on horse to carry the venison until I was weary of the business, which also gave me a taste for the forest. He resided on Crowder Creek until the year of 1768, his ardor for range and game still continued. He purchased a tract of land for one doubloon which at this time could not be purchased for five thousand dollars, such was the rapid increase of the value of land in half a century."—Felix Walker, first representative from Buncombe County to the United States Congress, on his early life on the Carolina frontier, in Walker, Memoirs of Hon. Felix Walker, *ed. Clarence Griffin (Forest City, N.C.: Forest City Courier, 1930)*

Frontier Agriculture

The primary occupation of most of the settlers across the great swath of hills and forest lands from western Virginia to the Carolina Piedmont was agriculture. Removed from the towns and commercial activity of Pennsylvania, the Scotch-Irish were now truly frontier pioneers. The type of agriculture they developed was shaped by the distinctive circumstances of the frontier as well as by the traditions of Ulster, for many were still very close to their Ulster origins. From their Ulster past they brought a heritage of dispersed settlements; a mixed farming in which both crops and livestock were raised; the use of simple tools; and an inefficient, even wasteful, use of the land. Circumstances settlers encountered in western Virginia and the Carolina Piedmont—a seemingly endless supply of cheap land, simple tools, few and often distant markets, and a constant shortage of labor—strongly encouraged the survival of those practices.

The backcountry was not completely forested when the early pioneers entered it. The Indians who had lived there for centuries had cleared much of it for cultivation. This was particularly so in the Valley of Virginia. Frequently, early white settlers could choose either to take over existing cleared areas ("old fields") or to clear their own. Though cleared land was preferred and might go for higher prices, the choice was not always obvious. Taking over cleared land meant plowing and manuring, a more intensive agriculture requiring a larger labor supply and aimed at selling to markets rather than family subsistence. Farming on uncleared land meant girdling and burning trees, depending on the natural fertility of the soil, and cultivating among the trees or stumps by hoe. As the soil wore out, "new ground" was cultivated and the process begun again. This slash-and-burn technique adopted from the Indians was well suited to a situation of plentiful land and scarce labor and was typical of the earliest frontier farming.

As for livestock, animals were allowed to graze on any land not fenced for crops, but primarily in the woods and upland pastures. They were branded or otherwise marked and then turned loose to fend for themselves. The great attraction of this method of stock raising was that it used uncleared land to produce a commercial commodity that could transport itself to distant markets. The great cattle drives to northern cities remained a major part of the rural economy throughout the eighteenth century.

The Scotch-Irish were not the only settlers who practiced this kind of frontier agriculture, for it was characteristic of the frontier South and particularly North Carolina. The anonymous author of *American Husbandry*, published in 1775, observed of North Carolina that "Such herds of cattle and swine are to be found in no other colonies, and when this is better settled,

Ludwig Gottfried von Redeken's early view of Salem, late eighteenth century. This Moravian community with its carefully fenced and cultivated fields and its dense settlement contrasts with the isolated pioneer farmstead. Photograph of painting reproduced courtesy Old Salem, Inc., Winston-Salem.

they will not be so common here: for at present the woods are all in common." He continued: "In this system of crops they change the land as fast as it wears out, clearing fresh pieces of woodland, exhausting them in succession, after which they leave them to spontaneous growth. . . . It presently becomes such wood as the rest of the country is: and woods here are the pasture of the cattle." This wasteful use of the land represented a modification of a traditional Ulster agriculture and preserved the single-family farm familiar to many Ulstermen. It presented a distinct contrast to the more intensive farming and highly organized villages of the English in New England and the Germans in Pennsylvania. At the same time, that frontier agriculture was highly flexible and became more efficient and commercial as land grew less plentiful and labor more available, and as markets became a more important part of farming life.

Presbyterianism and Politics on the Frontier

From the sixteenth century, Presbyterianism had shaped the lives of the Scotch-Irish. It formed a part of the mental outlook they brought to America and played an important role in the early communities they built. Though colonial governments did not encourage the growth of Presbyterianism and some, such as Virginia, supported an established Anglican Church, nonetheless toleration was widespread in the middle and southern colonies. The real challenge to Presbyterians was to sustain the practices of their faith on the expanding frontier.

While fostering good Calvinist virtues of individualism and self-sufficiency, the frontier did not necessarily nurture the other Christian virtues of kindness, compassion, and humility. The rough life of the frontier, away from the moral reinforcement of community, often rendered the Scotch-Irish wild and godless, at least in the often repeated view of contemporaries. Presbyterianism did not turn away from the task of carrying religion to its believers or to any others who would receive it. The faith sustained in Scotland and Ulster insisted upon a highly trained clergy that met rigorous standards of intellectual achievement in the arts and sciences as well as theology. It encouraged a literate community of believers who could read the Scriptures for themselves. Church governance also emphasized connectionalism, an organizational structure through which each church was directly connected to and subject to the supervision of a presbytery, which, along with other presbyteries, was governed by a synod. Collectively, these practices carried learning along the frontier, stimulated the growth of schools, and maintained the unity and strength of the church, tying the Presbyterian community together and nurturing and reinforcing its teachings.

Michel Guillaume Jean de Crèvecoeur feared the effects of the wild American frontier on settlers, warning that their lives were "regulated by the wildness of the neighborhood"; they became "ferocious, gloomy, and unsocial . . . no better than carnivorous animals of a superior rank, living on the flesh of wild animals."—Crèvecoeur, Letters from an American Farmer *(1782)*

The tightly organized structure of the Presbyterian Church did not work well on the frontier. As settlers moved further away, they advanced beyond the organizational capabilities of the church. It sometimes required years of petitioning before a presbytery could provide a pastor for a distant community. Still, Presbyterianism took root in the Valley of Virginia and the Carolina Piedmont and was the most visible manifestation of Scotch-Irish culture on the frontier. There the expansion of the frontier can be mapped by locating the founding of Presbyterian churches.

The growth of Presbyterianism south and west was largely the work of great missionary figures with strong ties to Pennsylvania. The first Presbyterian minister to settle in the Valley of Virginia was the Reverend John Craig, sent by the Donegal Presbytery (created in 1732) of Lancaster County, Pennsylania, to the Triple Forks of the Shenandoah River in 1740. Craig arrived in response to continuous petitions from people in the new communities of the Beverly Manor. He organized the Augusta Stone Church and the Tinkling Spring Church. Soon Augusta County was dotted with Presbyterian churches—some twenty-three by 1776—and had its own Presbytery of Abingdon.

The Reverend John Thomson was the first minister of any denomination to serve on the Yadkin frontier in North Carolina. Thomson was twice elected moderator of the General Synod of the Presbyterian Church and was the first moderator of the Donegal Presbytery. In 1744 his synod ordered him to correspond with the frontier people of North Carolina. He was apparently familiar with many of the settlers and in the early 1750s preached frequently at the meetinghouses of Thyatira and Centre and other places between the Yadkin and Catawba rivers. Though most of the growing number of congregations remained without resident ministers through the 1750s and 1760s, Carolina Presbyterianism took root and began to create its own schools and leadership. Representative of the quality and commitment of this new generation of clergy was James Hall, one of the great Carolina pastors and missionaries of his day. Hall's father left Ireland in 1730 and settled in Pennsylvania, where James was born in 1741. His family moved to Piedmont North Carolina in 1751. He graduated from Nassau Hall (later Princeton), served as a captain of cavalry and army chaplain during the Revolutionary War, and became a pastor in 1778 in what would soon be the Concord Presbytery. Rev. James Hall and the Scotch-Irish settlements of the western Piedmont, such as Quaker Meadows and Pleasant Gardens, played a major role in the birth of Presbyterianism in the North Carolina mountains.

Conflict on the Frontier

The coming of missionaries to the frontier communities was an event of great significance. The missionaries brought not only religion and learning but also news. In particular the ties of the frontier Scotch-Irish to Pennsylvania brought the political ideas and attitudes of that lively and progressive region into remote areas, in which they served as a political catalyst. Presbyterian clergy were closely associated with the spirit of independence and resistance to British rule. The clergy frequently found the people of the frontier deeply absorbed in local affairs and were not reluctant to bring radical politics to their congregations.

The Reverend Charles Woodmason, a Church of England clergyman, was alarmed by the growing resistance to British rule that he witnessed in the Carolina Piedmont in 1767: "Not less than 20 Itinerant Presbyterian, Baptist and Independent Preachers are maintain'd by the Synods of Pennsylvania and New England to traverse this Country Poisoning the Minds of the People—Instilling Democratical and Commonwealth Principles into their minds—Embittering them against the very name of Bishops, and all Episcopal Government and laying deep their fatal Republican Notions and Principles—Especially That they owe no Subjection to Great Britain—That they are a free People—That they are to pay allegiance to King George as their Sovereign—But as to Great Britain or the Parliament, or any there, that they have no more to think of or about them than the Turk or Pope— Thus do these Itinerant Preachers sent from the Northern Colonies pervert the Minds of the Vulgar."—Charles Woodmason, The Carolina Backcountry on the Eve of the Revolution, *ed. Richard J. Hooker (Chapel Hill: University of North Carolina Press, 1953)*

Scotch-Irish frontier communities had little reason to love the British government. It was the same government that had oppressed them in Ulster both economically and in religion. The Scotch-Irish brought with them from northern Ireland a suspicion of government and an attitude of resistance. Conditions in America encouraged them to thoughts of rebellion. By the 1760s the Scotch-Irish were caught up in armed struggle. Conflict between frontier communities and the colonial government in eastern North Carolina arose from the pioneers' beliefs that their interests were being ignored. Their resentment was expressed in the unsuccessful armed Regulator movement of 1771. Moreover, as populations grew in the backcountry, more settlers looked further west to the foothills and mountains. Their ambitions were blocked by Indians such as the Cherokees who lived there. The British government, in an effort to maintain peace with the Indians, had in 1763 established the Proclamation Line along the crest of the Appalachian Mountains. Though there were settlements west of the line, such as the Watauga community in East Tennessee, such settlements were illegal. The frontiersmen's desire to sweep away this British-protected barrier drew them into conflict with both Indians and the colonial government.

The most serious periods of conflict between whites and Indians along the North Carolina frontier occurred during the French and Indian War in the early 1760s and in the early years of the American Revolution. Indian raids were followed by punitive expeditions by whites pursuing a scorched-earth policy, which left Cherokee villages in ruins and the Indians forced to sue for peace. The most violent eighteenth-century clash on the North Carolina frontier came with the outbreak of the Revolution in 1776 and the Rutherford expedition. The British, following a long-established practice, attempted to use the Cherokees by stirring them to war against the rebellious settlers. With the memory of the French and Indian War still fresh, the Cherokees willingly responded. In response a colonial army commanded by Gen. Griffith Rutherford, an Ulsterman, marched across the Blue Ridge Mountains to punish the Indians and remove them as a threat. Many Scotch-Irish settlers, including the Reverend James Hall, marched with Rutherford and obtained their first glimpse of the Mountain region.

With the Indian menace reduced, the colonists were freed to devote their energies to the British threat. War stayed out of the South until 1780, when Cornwallis laid siege to Charleston as part of a plan to march inland through the backcountry, linking up with Loyalists along the way. Scotch-Irish settlers on the Carolina and Virginia frontier responded by employing hit-and-run raiding tactics learned from the Indians. Word of Cornwallis's depredations in South Carolina and the threat of his subordinate, Col. Patrick Ferguson, to destroy the Watauga settlements, spread throughout western North Carolina. In September 1780 men from Virginia, the Watauga settlements, and the Yadkin-Catawba region

Most of the men who fought on the American side at the Battle of Kings Mountain were Scotch-Irish settlers from the overmountain community of Watauga in Tennessee, from the North Carolina Piedmont, and from southwestern Virginia. Many of the veterans of the battle later settled in southwestern North Carolina. Illustration from Wilma Dykeman, *With Fire and Sword: The Battle of Kings Mountain* (Washington, D.C.: Office of Publications, National Park Service, U.S. Department of the Interior, 1978).

gathered at Quaker Meadows near Morganton and marched southeastward across the Blue Ridge to Charlotte. Near there, at Kings Mountain, South Carolina, they met Ferguson's army in battle and defeated it. That victory led to the retreat of Cornwallis from the Carolinas and ultimately to his voyage to Yorktown, where the military phase of the Revolution ended in 1781.

The Battle of Kings Mountain was significant for the North Carolina frontier in other ways as well. It ended the last serious threat of military disturbance in the mountains and made it a relatively peaceful and stable place for settlement. And, given the new North Carolina state government's practice of rewarding its Revolutionary veterans with land grants, it provided an impetus to further settlement, especially among veterans of the Rutherford expedition, who had seen firsthand the potential of the mountain frontier. Thus, victory in the Revolutionary War opened the way for a new surge of settlement into a rapidly westward-moving frontier.

5

Southwestern North Carolina: A Frontier Synthesis

At the close of the American Revolution, the new states quickly opened the territory west of the Blue Ridge and Allegheny Mountains to the first legal white settlement. Southwestern North Carolina was one of many regions along the spine of the Appalachians that now received a flood of people. For at least two decades those lands had been admired by men from the settlements of western Piedmont Carolina and Watauga in East Tennessee who hunted there or had accompanied General Rutherford to fight the Cherokees there in 1776. In the last years of the Revolutionary War, North Carolina passed legislation granting mountain lands to its veterans of the state's militia and the Continental army—from 640 acres for privates to 12,000 for brigadier generals. Others were allowed to buy mountain land cheaply throughout the period for five or ten cents per acre plus fees. A series of treaties with the Cherokees between 1785 and the 1830s made more land available and kept its price low. Beginning in 1787, when the first state grants were made on the Swannanoa and French Broad rivers, war veterans and others from the Piedmont and Watauga, as well as a steady flow of people down the Great Wagon Road, settled the mountain lands with surprising speed. Although early census figures are notorious for underestimating populations, the census of 1790 recorded 88 families, including some 559 individuals already settled on Reems Creek, and another considerable settlement to the south, where Bee Tree Creek enters the Swannanoa River.

Between 1787 and 1840 the Old West Frontier passed through southwestern North Carolina, and a new society evolved. The census of 1840 recorded a population of approximately thirty-four thousand people west of the eastern boundary of Buncombe County, including Buncombe, Henderson, Haywood, Macon, and Cherokee counties. Like all frontiers, the region was never static or isolated but was constantly growing and changing. For many new settlers, western North Carolina was only another temporary stop. These people grew a few crops on land they never legally claimed and then pushed on, westward into Tennessee and Kentucky or south to Georgia and Alabama. Some raised children before seeking a new home. Still others stayed. Those who settled among and frequently displaced the Cherokees were of diverse backgrounds—English, German, French, Welsh, and African American, as well as Scotch-Irish. No single ethnic group can claim an exclusive role in the creation of North Carolina's frontier mountain society, but a careful examination of surnames and family histories in the new communities indicates that the largest group among the early settlers, perhaps one-third of them, was the Scotch-Irish.

The Scotch-Irish Community

There have been several attempts to determine the ethnic origins of America's early settlers. The task is a difficult one, and all efforts have provoked criticism and doubt. Examination of a reasonably small community allows for greater certainty but still yields results that can be only approximate. Because people have migrated within the British Isles and Ireland for thousands of years, it is difficult to identify Scotch-Irish names. For example, Smith was the most common name in both Scotland and Ireland in the nineteenth century. The following figures represent a conservative minimum estimate; the actual numbers may easily be as much as 15 percent higher.

The census returns of 1790 and 1800 for the small communities west of the Blue Ridge Mountains show that a very high percentage of families were of Ulster origins—40 percent of 88 families in 1790 and 43 percent of 888 families in 1800. As the frontier moved west, the percentage slowly declined: in the 1810 census for the new county of Haywood, 32 percent of the 384 families bore Ulster names; in the new county of Macon in 1830, 31 percent of 813 families did so; and in the 1840 census of the westernmost county of Cherokee, 25 percent of 501 families were distinctly Scotch-Irish. These minimal estimates suggest that the earliest settlers of the region were drawn from large concentrations of Scotch-Irish immigrants who had traveled down the Great Wagon Road into the Carolina Piedmont and the Watauga settlement of East Tennessee in the thirty years before the Revolution. Those two areas served as population reservoirs from which southwestern North Carolina drew its first inhabitants, men who had hunted and fought in the mountains and knew the land well. The high percentage of Scotch-Irish in the two areas gradually declined as many of those people dispersed—moving into western North Carolina and onward—and were replaced by newcomers of more varied ethnic backgrounds. These estimates for southwestern North Carolina are considerably higher than those for the state as a whole, which a 1931 study set at only 11 percent. The relative size of the Scotch-Irish community in the mountain counties declined as migration into and out of the region continued after the initial period.

The impression that the Scotch-Irish community was large and important yet changing during the frontier period is supported by the role of the Scotch-Irish in community leadership. More than 60 percent of the resident landowners in Buncombe and Haywood counties who owned more than one thousand acres between 1788 and 1810 were Scotch-Irish. Ten of sixteen landowners in the new town of Asheville had names and family histories indicating Ulster origins. Half the justices of the peace and five of seven officeholders for Buncombe County in 1792 were Scotch-Irish. But by the 1840s and 1850s in newly settled Cherokee County, only 35 percent of the men who served as justices of the peace bore Scotch-Irish names.

During the first fifty years of settlement, the Scotch-Irish element in western North Carolina was in flux, as might be expected from the restless nature of the group; but it formed a substantial minority in a growing, evolving society, and its social prominence exceeded its size. Early family histories verify this: Felix Walker, whose father emigrated from County Derry in 1720, served three terms in the United States House of Representatives; David Vance, one of the first men to settle across the Blue Ridge, was a member of the North Carolina House of Commons, a founder of Buncombe County, and grandfather of a governor of North Carolina; Robert Henry was a teacher, surveyor, lawyer, physician, historian, and writer; James Patton, whom we met in Pennsylvania, was an early Asheville merchant, and his partner, Andrew Erwin, was a member of the North Carolina House of Commons.

This large, mobile, and adaptive group of immigrants brought to their new homes a culture formed in Scotland and the north of Ireland and shaped by an ongoing process of migration. They had put aside much of their Ulster legacy for new ways with few signs of regret. The Scotch-Irish brought a simple, practical, and unadorned style of life, but in at least two essential areas—religion and agriculture—their mark upon mountain life still bears witness to their Ulster origins.

"These mountains [of North Carolina] begin to be populated rapidly. The salubrity of the air, the excellence of the water, and more especially the pasturage of these wild peas for the cattle, are so many causes that induce new inhabitants to settle there.

"Estates of the first class are sold at the rate of two dollars, and the taxes are not more than a half-penny per acre. Indian corn, wheat, rye, oats, and peach trees, are the sole object of culture.

"The inhabitants of these mountains are famed for being excellent hunters. Towards the middle of autumn most of them go in pursuit of bears, of which they sell the skins, and the flesh, which is very good, serves them in great measure for food during that season. They prefer it to all other kinds of meat, and look upon it as the only thing they can eat without being indisposed by it. They make also of their hind legs the most delicious hams. . . . They hunt them with great dogs, which, without going near them, bark, tease, and oblige them to climb up a tree, when the hunter kills them with a carbine." Francis Andre Michaux, Travels to the Westward of the Allegany Mountains *(London, 1805)*

Presbyterianism in the Mountains

Presbyterianism had traveled far with the Scotch-Irish and remained the most visible manifestation of their Ulster background. The Presbyterian Church appeared in the history of mountain settlement almost as early as the Scotch-Irish themselves, although its organization and administration were haphazard and uncertain. Initially the westernmost area of North Carolina came under the supervision of the Abingdon Presbytery, organized in 1786, which also covered southwestern Virginia and the Watauga settlement. Burke and Rutherford counties were administered by the Concord Presbytery of the Carolina Synod. But just as most of the Scotch-Irish immigrants entered the Blue Ridge Mountains from the Piedmont, so too did the Presbyterian Church. The birthing and nurturing of the earliest congregations in mountain settlements were largely the work of Piedmont Carolinians.

The central figure in this work was the great frontier missionary James Hall, who first preached in the mountains of North Carolina in 1790. According to the minutes of the General Assembly of the Presbyterian Church for 1797, three churches had been founded in 1794 in the Asheville area of Buncombe County: the Reems Creek, Swannanoa, and Head of the French Broad River congregations. But James Hall's report to the Synod of the Carolinas in October

1793, describing his recent visit to Buncombe County, indicates that the congregations were established at least as early as 1790, though without resident clergy. In 1797 the Reverend George Newton, born in in 1765 in York County, Pennsylvania, left Piedmont North Carolina to accept a call from the united congregations of Swannanoa and Reems Creek. Subsequently the Reverend Mr. Newton was instrumental in the formation of other Presbyterian churches farther west: Armageddon Church in the Turkey Creek, Sandy Mush, and New Foord areas, and Bethsalem Church in the Pigeon River and Richland Creek area.

Also in the early 1790s the Scotch-Irish Presbyterians of Buncombe County established an academy near the mouth of the Swannanoa River on land owned by William Forster, who was born in Ireland in 1748. Robert Henry, of Scotch-Irish descent and a veteran of the Battle of Kings Mountain, taught in this first North Carolina school west of the Blue Ridge. In 1797 George Newton assumed direction of the academy, which was later named for him. The curriculum offered Greek and Latin, as well as basic skills, and produced from among its early students a governor of North Carolina and a governor of South Carolina. The trustees of the academy comprised a roster of the regional elite, many Scotch-Irish among them. In 1810 a group of prominent citizens interested in "literary advancement" undertook an enterprise for Newton Academy that became famous in the history of western North Carolina. They organized a lottery with a seven thousand-dollar prize to raise money with which to establish a female academy in Asheville, but it failed, "owing to the extreme scarcity of cash," and the money was refunded.

It was not only the Scotch-Irish ideal of learning that was difficult to sustain on the Carolina frontier; the Presbyterian Church also experienced difficulty in maintaining its congregations in Scotch-Irish society. In 1809, following a tour of the churches in the region, the Reverend James Hall reported that "respecting the State of religion it is not as in years past." He deplored the disastrous impact of the Great Awakening that had swept the Carolinas early in the nineteenth century with its "most wild and delusive fanaticism" and its "horrid and extravagant conduct." He also bemoaned the lack of ministers, a consequence of the Presbyterian insistence that its clergy be educated in seminaries: "Our vacant churches in those counties, still look up to us, for public instructions and the administrations of the sealing ordinances of the Gospel; but lament that they have from us too few supplies. On this account

The Great Awakening that swept the American frontier in the first decade of the nine-teenth century introduced the camp meeting as an important feature of the religious life of small scattered communities. It also marked a sharp decline of Presbyterianism among the Scotch-Irish community. Drawing from Thomas H. Clayton, *Close to the Land: The Way We Lived in North Carolina, 1820–1870* (Chapel Hill: University of North Carolina Press for the North Carolina Department of Cultural Resources, 1983), 51.

in sundry places, from principles of necessity, they employ preachers of other denominations to impart to them, some of their ministerial labours. For this and other causes, our members are dropping off, and our societies annually melting away; so that unless some remedy be afforded they will ere long cease to exist." Given the paucity of Scottish and Irish Presbyterian clergymen who emigrated to America and the scarcity of Presbyterian seminaries in the New World, mountain congregations found it almost impossible to obtain trained clergymen to minister to them.

The shortage of qualified ministers was complicated by the remoteness of the mountain counties from the center of the presbytery in the Piedmont and by the emphasis upon connectionalism. Presbyterianism west of the Blue Ridge did not flourish under those circumstances. The congregations of Armageddon and Bethsalem appear to have had a short life—they were heard from no more after their founding. Between 1805 and 1813, Newton attended only one meeting of the presbytery; and when he left Buncombe County for Tennessee in 1813, he was not replaced for four years. Despite those difficulties, the original church in Buncombe County and the academy in Asheville did survive. Presbyterianism was able to maintain a presence across the western counties and an identification with the Scotch-Irish community throughout the period. That presence, however, was greatly reduced after about 1810 by the rapid growth of Baptist and Methodist churches in the mountains, and there is no doubt that the absence of qualified Presbyterian clergy caused many old Scotch-Irish families to join those denominations rather than to abandon religious life altogether.

Presbyterianism experienced a renewal of activity in the 1820s associated with the work of the Reverend Christopher Bradshaw. Bradshaw first served in the southern part of Buncombe County, where in 1828 he organized the Davidson River Church, with three elders and twenty-seven members. Sixty-five new members had been added by 1834, and by 1836 an academy was associated with the church. In 1833 Bradshaw was involved in the organization of the Franklin Presbyterian Church in Macon County, which recorded 101 members in 1836 but was inactive by the 1840s. In 1834 the Reverend William Hall reported that he had founded a church in Haywood County to be known as the Ebenezer Church. And in 1841 Rev. Christopher Bradshaw organized in newly created Cherokee County a congregation known as the Hiwassee Church and moved west to serve it. Hiwassee was small and grew slowly, but it survived. The session books of the Davidson River and Hiwassee Churches have also survived and provide a list of elders and members. There is no mistaking the Scotch-Irish identity of these congregations and their role as the core of a small continuing Presbyterian presence within the region. But the great majority of the Scotch-Irish had found new religious loyalties. By the early 1840s there were only seven Presbyterian churches serving fewer than three hundred members across southwestern North Carolina. In comparison, thirty-seven Baptist congregations and thirty-two Methodist ones were listed in the region in the census of 1850.

While Presbyterian congregations declined in numbers and in importance in western North Carolina, Presbyterian religious practices survived and greatly influenced the development of religion in the mountains. The Scottish and Ulster tradition of sacramental or holy fairs was especially important, and James McGready was representative of the clergymen who developed it in America during the Great Awakening. McGready, of Scotch-Irish descent, was born in Pennsylvania and raised in Guilford County, North Carolina. There he encouraged the Scottish practice of coming together in open fields to renew one's covenant with God. His holy fairs included fasting on Thursdays or Fridays; preparation to receive communion on Saturdays; Sunday exercises consisting of prayer, psalm singing, sermons, and communion; and a final service of thanksgiving on Mondays. Accompanying devotional practices included prayer, self-examination, devotional readings, and meditation. Renewal of one's covenant with God involved renunciation of temptation and sin, acceptance of Christ, rededication to God, and renewal of the baptismal covenant. Ecstatic experiences including trances, fainting spells, supernatural voices, and visions commonly occurred during those occasions. While conservative clergymen like James Hall feared the emotions released during those fairs and attacked them as superstitious and licentious, they created a sense of community that helped bind dispersed frontier settlers together. These Scotch-Irish religious practices left an enduring mark on the development of religious revivalism in the mountains.

Mountain Agriculture

Besides religion, the other aspect of mountain life on which the Scotch-Irish left an enduring mark was their use of the land. They brought their pattern of mixed farming with them, and they found it well suited to their new environment. This mixed farming was appropriate for the mountains because it did not require large amounts of first-quality land and could in fact utilize unclaimed "open range." Nor did it require the amount of capital that was needed to obtain the best lands, so it was better suited to immigrants who had left Ulster with little material wealth. And it was appropriate to a heavily forested region that suffered from a long-term shortage of labor.

This type of mixed farming is described in the wills and farm inventories of the earliest settlers, such as those surviving for Haywood County before the Civil War. Grains were the dominant crops, with Indian corn far and away the leader, followed by oats, wheat, and barley. Plows are listed in most of the inventories, indicating that in addition to hoe cultivation many fields were also

A family planting corn at Linville Falls, North Carolina, May 1905, employing agricultural practices developed in the pioneer period. Photograph courtesy North Carolina Collection, Wilson Library, University of North Carolina at Chapel Hill.

being cleared of stumps and plowed as agriculture moved out of the earliest pioneer slash-and-burn phase. Other crops such as flax and cotton were also grown, though in small amounts and for household use.

That type of agriculture, which depended upon slash-and-burn techniques to remove trees and the hoe to cultivate around the remaining stumps, as well as the raising of small numbers of animals, was a pattern that had been practiced in Ulster in the infield-outfield system, and it was a pattern that the Scotch-Irish stamped upon the mountains of western North Carolina.

The Haywood County wills and inventories also list animals, including hogs, cattle, horses, and sheep, but not in large numbers. In his study of colonial North Carolina, Roy Merrens points out that during the 1780s, when Piedmont settlers were driving large numbers of cattle to northern markets, the average size of herds was 6 to 16 head. In southwestern North Carolina, hogs were the most common livestock raised, the average holding being 22 hogs, with 7 farms listing more than 30. Cattle were held in smaller numbers, with an average holding of 8 cattle and only a few farms listing more than 20. Sheep, listed in only half of the wills and inventories, averaged 6 per farm. Economic

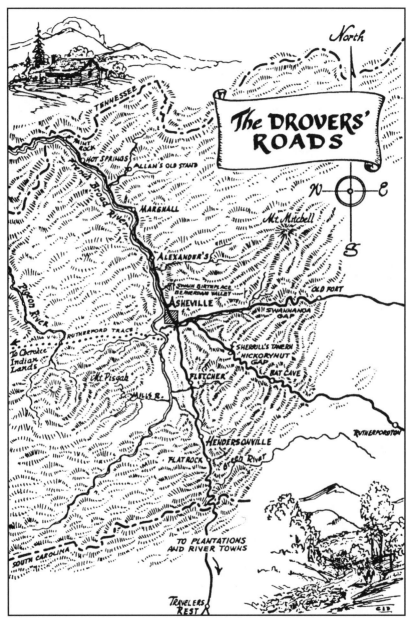

The Drovers' Road ran from Greeneville, Tennessee, through southwestern North Carolina to Greenville, South Carolina, connecting the region to Charleston and Savannah and to the larger American economy. It was a route of settlement in the early nineteenth century as well as the site of the great cattle and hog drives that were so important to the region's economy. Map from Clifford R. Lovin, ed., *Our Mountain Heritage: Essays on the Natural and Cultural History of Western North Carolina* (Cullowhee: Mountain Heritage Center, 1979), 90.

data compiled for the agricultural census of 1850 confirms the small numbers of animals. In Cherokee County, where the land had been open to white settlement only since 1838, the numbers of animals were quite comparable to those listed in the Haywood wills and inventories, the average holding being 27 hogs, 14 cattle, and 11 sheep.

But the agricultural economy of the mountain frontier was never one of isolated subsistence. From the beginning, merchants penetrated the mountain frontier, and the settlers maintained some connection, however slight at first, to an outside market economy. The experience of James Patton, the weaver from County Derry, offers a valuable insight into the commercial aspect of the frontier economy. Patton knew little about farm work and had no taste for it. In the Philadelphia area he found various employment as a casual laborer until in 1789 he had accumulated enough money to purchase a stock of dry goods and set out as a drummer, or traveling merchant, for western North Carolina. That initial foray marked the beginning of his new career carrying merchandise south to the North Carolina mountains and driving livestock north to the cities of Washington, Baltimore, and Philadelphia.

"This summer I intended to go to Philadelphia to dispose of my furs, and purchase goods to enable me to buy a handsome drove of cattle, but finding it would be too late before I could go and return, I stopped at Staunton, Augusta County, Virginia, and employed three hatters to work up a part of my fur into hats, and paid them in fur for their labors. I returned to North Carolina with my hats in boxes, packed on horses. I purchased all the cattle I was able to pay for, in the counties of Wilkes, Burke and Buncombe, and started for Philadelphia; stopped at Staunton, Virginia, and took on the balance of the furs which I had left there. I purchased in Philadelphia as many goods as I was able to pay for, and returned to North Carolina with two wagons, one loaded with goods, and the other with my mother and family [who had arrived shortly before from Ireland]."—Letter of James Patton, describing his commercial ventures in 1792

Patton's experiences offer a good idea of what it took to prosper as a merchant working on the frontier and also illustrate that western North Carolina was not isolated from the outside market economy. The primary "cash crop" that mountaineers raised for the market was livestock, chiefly hogs, which according to Patton were driven out of the mountains in large numbers by traders like himself. Other market commodities that he bought from mountain farmers included furs, feathers, beeswax, and roots for medicine such as ginseng and snakeroot. Among the goods he carried into the mountains were cotton clothing and fabrics, buckles, buttons, and silver lockets. Other merchants brought hardware; cotton cloth; shoes; drugs; bonnets; silk goods; and a wide range of books, including Bibles, histories, biographies, almanacs, dictionaries, and books of etiquette. Those commodities were exchanged with dealers in a network that included cities as far away as Boston.

During his life Patton saw economic activity grow from the late 1780s, when there was little money available in the mountains, to the 1830s, when his inventories of trade goods reveal a significant expansion of commerce. He later wrote: "I settled in the upper part of North Carolina at that time the poorest part of the country I ever saw to make property; but I do not entertain the same opinion now. Changes and improvements have convinced me that there are few sections of the country superior to the western part of North Carolina." Allowing for regional pride, Patton's narrative records the steady if not rapid development of the southwestern counties since the 1790s and the emergence of an economy of small farms increasingly engaging in commercialized mixed farming.

This examination of the changing dimensions of the Scotch-Irish element in antebellum southwestern North Carolina suggests a numerous and still identifiable people but one rapidly and quite willingly blending into their cultural surroundings. By 1840 ethnic identities were largely submerged in rural mountain culture by the appearance of new generations and new people. Yet, there still lived a few settlers who had personal memories of a home across the ocean. James Patton lived until September 1845. The census of 1850, the first to record place of birth, lists Fannie Love Ferguson, widow of Robin Ferguson and one of the first settlers in the Crabtree community of Haywood County, still alive at seventy-eight. Beside her name is the notation "born Tirone County, Ireland."

The Carson House was begun in 1793 by Col. John Carson at Pleasant Gardens in the Catawba valley. When McDowell County was created in 1843, the Carson House served as the seat of county government until a courthouse was constructed. The original two-story log structure reached its present form by the middle of the nineteenth century. Photograph from the files of the Office of Archives and History.

"I doubt not that those [Scotch-Irish] pioneers who came to the South and gave all their strength and devotion to the fabrication of such civilization as we have were grim and determined and stiff-necked and opinionated and fearless people. It is probably easier to admire them than it would have been pleasant to live with them. I spent my earliest days amongst them and I have no doubt that their attributes had been transmitted almost unmodified to them by their ancestors for generation after generation. They were and they are undemonstrative, apparently without affection and superficially cold. But they generally have opinions, right or wrong, and they are altogether willing, if not anxious, to stand by their opinions to their last breaths. I scarcely think our government could have come into being without them."— Personal correspondence of J. K. Hall, describing in 1941 his Scotch-Irish ancestors in North Carolina (Pennsylvania Historical Society, Philadelphia)

COL. JOHN
CARSON
SON OF
JAMES &
REBECCA
HAZARD
CARSON
BORN IN
COUNY
FERMANAGH,
IRELAND
MAR. 24, 1752
TWICE MARRIED
FIRST TO
RACHEL
McDOWELL
SECOND WIFE
MARY
McDOWELL
NEE MOFFETT
DIED
MAR. 5, 1841

Col. John Carson was an Ulsterman from County Fermanagh and a pioneer of the upper Catawba valley. He was a representative to the Fayetteville Convention of 1789, in which North Carolina ratified the United States Constitution. He also served in the North Carolina House of Commons from 1805 to 1806. The gravestone is located in McDowell County in the Round Hill Cemetery, Pleasant Gardens, N.C., (GPS 35.705062-82.046844). GPS information courtesy of Donna Thomas.

Conclusion

Two hundred years have passed since James Patton left Ulster on the travels that would bring him and his family to southwestern North Carolina. It has been almost as many years since Samuel Davidson left his home in the Catawba valley to establish the first white settlement across the Blue Ridge Mountains in North Carolina. His death at the hands of angry Cherokees did not dissuade tens of thousands of others from following him as the land was opened over the next five decades. The Scotch-Irish moved at the front of the wave of pioneers who filled the rich river bottoms and settled along the small creeks and hollows. Many did not stay for long; the mountains of North Carolina represented for them only another stop as they moved west and south to pioneer the upper South and the trans-Appalachian region.

In those areas too the search for the Scotch-Irish continues as historians, genealogists, and those interested in their local history attempt to identify and evaluate this elusive people who played such a vital role in early American history. Professors Forrest McDonald and Grady McWhiney have argued in a series of recent studies that southern history has been profoundly influenced by the presence of a large "Celtic" majority. They maintain that this group, predominantly Scotch-Irish, brought to the South distinctive attitudes and traditions: a rowdy rebelliousness; a suspicion of authority in all forms; and an agriculture that disdained tillage of the soil and concentrated upon herding and hunting, leaving the individual to enjoy a leisure time that bordered on indolence. Their ideas have provoked heated debate, and most scholars agree that McDonald and McWhiney have greatly exaggerated their thesis.

Two fundamental features of the early Scotch-Irish do stand out. The first is the cultural interaction they experienced with people around them throughout their migrations. They never settled in isolation from others. The second is their readiness to change and adopt new ideas and practices. Perhaps their most persistent trait as settlers on the American frontier was their way of using the land, evolved in the uplands of Scotland and Ireland and ideally suited to the frontier that unfolded south and west of Pennsylvania in the eighteenth and nineteenth centuries. Their familiarity, even contentment, with that way of life drew them to the frontier and invited them ever onward in search of plentiful land and game. Their preference for the single-family farm over the village community sustained

their strong spirit of individuality and the importance of family and self-sufficiency. This is where their greatest influence lies—in the land-use and social organization they brought to much of the South. The open-range system, in which crops were fenced and livestock roamed free, prevailed across much of the South into the twentieth century and is an important element in the shaping of southern history.

By the mid-nineteenth century, there had developed in southwestern North Carolina a society that was a synthesis of cultures and peoples responding to their new environment. That new Appalachian culture was shaped by forces distinct to the region. Ethnicity was largely submerged by regional conflicts within the state; by new economic activities such as logging, mining, and tourism; by the intervention of the federal government in land policies and development projects; and by continuing in- and out-migration as the southern Appalachians became increasingly differentiated from surrounding regions. Those who would understand modern Appalachia are right to pursue these themes; but a true understanding of the traditions of the region and its sense of itself still calls us back to the ethnic heritages that the first settlers brought.

Selected Bibliography

Blethen, H. Tyler, and Curtis W. Wood Jr. "A Trader on the Western Carolina Frontier." In *Appalachian Frontiers: Settlement, Society, & Development in the Preindustrial Era*, ed. Robert D. Mitchell. Lexington: University Press of Kentucky, 1990, 150–165.

_____, eds. *Ulster and North America: Transatlantic Perspectives on the Scotch-Irish*. Tuscaloosa: University of Alabama Press, 1997.

Bolton, C. K. *Scotch Irish Pioneers in Ulster and America*. Boston: Bacon and Brown, 1910.

Brooke, Peter. *Ulster Presbyterianism: The Historical Perspective, 1610–1970*. Dublin: Gill and Macmillan, 1987.

Campbell, John C. *The Southern Highlander and His Homeland*. Lexington: University Press of Kentucky, 1921; reprinted 1969.

Crawford, W. H. "Landlord-Tenant Relations in Ulster, 1609–1820." *Irish Economic and Social History* 2 (1975): 5–21.

Dickson, D. *New Foundations: Ireland 1660–1800*. Dublin: Gill and Macmillan, 1987.

Dickson, R. J. *Ulster Emigration to Colonial America, 1718–1775*. Belfast: Ulster Historical Association, 1966; reprinted Belfast: Ulster Historical Association, 1988.

Doyle, David N. *Ireland, Irishmen and Revolutionary America, 1760–1820*. Cork and Dublin: Mercier Press, 1981.

Evans, E. Estyn. "Cultural Relics of the Ulster Scots in the Old West of North America." *Ulster Folklife* 11 (1965): 33–38.

_____. "The Scotch-Irish: Their Cultural Adaptation and Heritage in the American Old West." In *Essays in Scotch-Irish History*, ed. E. R. R. Green. London: Routledge & Kegan Paul, 1969.

Fischer, David Hackett. *Albion's Seed: Four British Folkways in America*. New York: Oxford University Press, 1989.

Fitzpatrick, Rory. *God's Frontiersmen: The Scots-Irish Epic*. London: Weidenfeld and Nicolson, 1989.

Ford, H. J. *The Scotch-Irish in America*. Princeton: Princeton University Press, 1915.

Gillespie, Raymond. *Colonial Ulster: The Settlement of East Ulster 1600–1641*. Cork: Cork University Press, 1985.

Glassie, Henry. *Patterns in the Material Folk Culture of the Eastern United States*. Philadelphia: University of Pennsylvania Press, 1968.

Green, E. R. R., ed. *Essays in Scotch-Irish History*. London: Routledge & Kegan Paul, 1969.

Hanna, C. A. *The Scotch-Irish*. 2 vols. New York: G. P. Putnam and Sons, 1902; reprinted Baltimore: Genealogical Publishing Co., 1968.

Jones, Maldwyn A. "The Scotch-Irish in British America." In *Strangers within the Realm: Cultural Margins of the First British Empire*, ed. Bernard Bailyn and Philip D. Morgan. Chapel Hill: University of North Carolina Press, 1991.

Keller, Kenneth W. "What Is Distinctive about the Scotch-Irish?" In *Appalachian Frontiers*, ed. Robert D. Mitchell. Lexington: University Press of Kentucky, 1991.

Kephart, Horace. *Our Southern Highlanders*. New York: Macmillan, 1922.

Lemon, James T. *The Best Poor Man's Country: A Geographical Study of Early Southeastern Pennsylvania*. Baltimore: Johns Hopkins University Press, 1972.

Leyburn, James G. *The Scotch-Irish: A Social History*. Chapel Hill: University of North Carolina Press, 1962.

McDonald, Forrest, and Ellen Shapiro McDonald. "The Ethnic Origins of the American People, 1790." *William and Mary Quarterly* 37 (April 1980): 179–199.

McDonald, Forrest, and Grady McWhiney. "The Antebellum Southern Herdsman: A Reinterpretation." *Journal of Southern History* 41 (May 1975): 147–166.

_____. "Celtic Origins of Southern Herding Practices." *Journal of Southern History* 51 (May 1985): 165–182.

McWhiney, Grady. *Cracker Culture: Celtic Ways in the Old South.* Tuscaloosa: University of Alabama Press, 1988.

Michaux, Francis Andre. *Travels to the Westward of the Allegany Mountains.* London, 1805.

Miller, Kerby. *Emigrants and Exiles: Ireland and the Irish Exodus to North America.* New York: Oxford University Press, 1985.

Mitchell, Robert D. *Commercialism and Frontier: Perspectives on the Early Shenandoah Valley.* Charlottesville: University of Virginia Press, 1972.

Mitchison, R., and P. Roebuck, eds. *Economy and Society in Scotland and Ireland, 1500–1939.* Edinburgh: John Donald Press, 1988.

Montgomery, Michael. "The Roots of Appalachian English: Scotch-Irish or British Southern?" *Journal of the Appalachian Studies Association* 3 (1991): 177–191.

Moody, T. W., F. X. Martin, and F. J. Byrne, eds. *A New History of Ireland: III, Early Modern Ireland, 1534–1691.* Oxford: Clarendon Press, 1976.

Otto, John Solomon. *The Southern Frontier, 1607–1860: The Agricultural Evolution of the Colonial and Antebellum South.* New York: Greenwood Press, 1989.

Perceval-Maxwell, M. *The Scottish Migration to Ulster in the Reign of James I.* Belfast: Ulster Historical Foundation, 1990.

Purvis, Thomas L. "The European Ancestry of the United States Population, 1790." *William and Mary Quarterly* 41 (January 1984): 85–101.

Robinson, Philip. *The Plantation of Ulster: British Settlement in an Irish Landscape, 1600–1700.* New York: St. Martin's Press, 1984.

Truxes, T. M. *Irish-American Trade, 1600–1783.* Cambridge: Cambridge University Press, 1988.

Westerkamp, Marilyn Jeanne. *Triumph of the Laity: Scots-Irish Piety and the Great Awakening, 1625–1760.* New York: Oxford University Press, 1988.

Index

A

Abingdon Presbytery (Va.), 47, 55
Africans/African Americans,
    19, 53
Agriculture: infield/outfield
    system of, 8–9, 60; mixed, 1;
    in North Carolina mountains,
    59–62; in North Carolina
    Piedmont, 43–45; practices
    of, by Indians, 44; practices
    of, by Scotch–Irish, 31, 34,
    44–45; in Scotland, 6–9; slash-
    and-burn method of, 44,
    59–60; in Ulster, 7–9, 18–19
Alabama, 53
Alexander, Thomas, 24
Allan, Samuel, 24
Allegheny Mountains,
    35, 37, 39, 52
Allen, John, 25
America (ship), 23
American Husbandry (book), 44
American Revolution, 20, 47,
    49, 52
Anglican Church, 10,
    11, 14–15, 46
Anglicans, 20
Annapolis, Md., 25
Antrim. *See* County Antrim
Appalachian Mountains,
    xiv, 38, 49, 52, 67
Armageddon Church, 56, 57
Armagh. *See* County Armagh
Ash, J., 25
Ash, Thomas, 25

Asheville, N.C.: church founded
    in the area of, 55; early
    residents of, 22, 33, 54;
    female academy at, 56, 58
Atlantic passage, 22–26
Augusta County (Va.),
    38, 39, 41, 47, 62
Augusta Stone Church, 47

B

Baker, James, 25
Bally Castle, ii
Ballymoney, 16
Baltimore, Md., 25, 62
Bangor (Ulster parish), 7
Bann Valley, 17
Baptists, 48, 58
Battle of Kings Mountain, 50, 51,
    56
Bee Tree Creek, 52
Belfast (Ulster port), 20, 23, 24, 25
Belfast *News Letter*, 20, 21, 24
Bell, Robert, 24
Bethsalem Church, 56, 58
Betsy (ship), 25
Betty (ship), 25
Beverly, William, 39
Beverly Manor (Va.), 35, 38, 39, 47
Blair, Robert, 7
Blue Mountains, 35
Blue Ridge Mountains: first white
    settlement established across,
    66; passage through, 41; Pres-
    byterianism west of, 57; Ruth-
    erford marched across, 49, 51;